ARCHITECTURE
IN NEW ENGLAND

CHARLES BULFINCH, CHURCH OF CHRIST, LANCASTER, MASSACHUSETTS, 1816

ARCHITECTURE
IN
NEW ENGLAND

A Photographic History

WAYNE ANDREWS

ICON EDITIONS

HARPER & ROW, PUBLISHERS

NEW YORK

Cambridge   London
Hagerstown   Mexico City
Philadelphia São Paulo
San Francisco Sydney

1817

BOOKS BY WAYNE ANDREWS

Siegfried's Curse: The German Journey from Nietzsche to Hesse   1972

Architecture in New York: A Photographic History   1969

Architecture in Chicago and Mid-America   1968

Architecture in Michigan   1967

Germaine: A Portrait of Madame de Staël   1963

Architecture in America   1960

Best Short Stories of Edith Wharton (editor)   1958

Architecture, Ambition and Americans   1955

Who Has Been Tampering with These Pianos?   1948
  (under the pseudonym Montagu O'Reilly)

Battle for Chicago   1946

The Vanderbilt Legend   1941

ARCHITECTURE IN NEW ENGLAND: A PHOTOGRAPHIC HISTORY. Copyright © 1973 by Wayne Andrews. All rights reserved. Printed in the United States of America. No part of this book may be used or reproduced in any manner whatsoever without written permission except in the case of brief quotations embodied in critical articles and reviews. For information address Harper & Row, Publishers, Inc., 10 East 53rd Street, New York, N.Y. 10022. Published simultaneously in Canada by Fitzhenry & Whiteside Limited, Toronto.

First Icon Edition published in 1980.

ISBN: 0-06-430106-0
LIBRARY OF CONGRESS CATALOG CARD NUMBER: 80-7766

80 81 82 83 10 9 8 7 6 5 4 3 2 1

Contents

Acknowledgments

A grant from the American Philosophical Society was most helpful in the final stages of the photography for this book. My fellow architectural historians Alan Burnham, Leonard K. Eaton, William H. Jordy, and George B. Tatum were so kind as to give me their best advice, and I am also indebted to many other people, in particular to: Louis S. Auchincloss, Carl Bridenbaugh, Richard M. Candee of Old Sturbridge, Abbott L. Cummings of the Society for the Preservation of New England Antiquities and his associate Richard C. Nylander, Louise Dresser of the Worcester Art Museum, Malcolm Freiberg of the Massachusetts Historical Society, Donald T. Gibbs of the Redwood Library, James J. Heslin of the New-York Historical Society, Melancthon W. Jacobus of the Connecticut Historical Society, Philip Monteleoni, Mrs. Thomas D. Mumford, Headmistress of the Foxhollow School, Albert L. Nickerson, John F. Page of the New Hampshire Historical Society, Charles Shipman Payson, Mrs. Gilbert R. Payson of the Essex Institute, A. K. Placzek of Avery Library, Charles A. Platt II, Eliot T. Putnam, Headmaster Emeritus of the Noble & Greenough School, Theodore A. Sande of the Society for Industrial Archeology, Alexander J. Wall of Old Sturbridge, Walter Muir Whitehill of the Boston Athenaeum and his associate Jack Jackson, and Cynthia Zaitzevsky.

And I should mention Dick Schuler, Ernest Pile, and Sybil Collins of Compo Photocolor, New York, who have developed and printed my negatives for so long and given me such good advice.

Finally, Stephen and Janet Greene have shared with me their great knowledge of New England.

Foreword

NEW ENGLAND — or at least rural New England — may be described as the place most Americans would like to live if they did not have to earn their livings elsewhere. This means that a certain nostalgia hangs over the area. Here are the towns, here is the countryside to which Americans like to retreat when made too uncomfortable over what has gone wrong in their world.

Of course not every American shares this reverence for New England. Edith Wharton, for example, had her misgivings. Speaking as the creator of *Ethan Frome,* she decided that New England was "a vision of earnest women in Shetland shawls, with spectacles and thin knobs of hair, eating blueberry pie at unwholesome hours in a shingled dining-room."

The merits of blueberry pie are none of our business at the moment, but Mrs. Wharton would certainly agree that the architecture of New England has its importance. A number of masterpieces are still there to remind us that in the age of Charles Bulfinch as in the age of H. H. Richardson this area led the nation. These masterpieces have not been forgotten by the author of this book. If they are not all included, it is for want of space. But if the important is important, so is the typical: a genuine effort has been made to reveal what is considered, rightly or wrongly, the genuine article. The saltboxes of Cape Cod have not been overlooked. Neither have the covered bridges and round barns of Vermont nor the mills of Lowell and Manchester. And to prove how stubbornly conservative New England may be at times, there is the tiny town hall of Royalton, Vermont. Although erected in 1840, it has the character of forty years before. Fortunately, there is also a certain amount of bad taste in this book. What one generation insists is the bad taste of another is bound,

sooner or later, to come into its own. Or, as the subtle English critic Geoffrey Scott observed, whatever has been found to be genuinely pleasing is likely to be found pleasing once again.

This is not a book about New England pure and undefiled, the kind of thing that the Cotton Mathers of every generation would endorse. The palaces of Newport are given their due, even though they represent a surrender to the millionaires from New York. And there is a place here for Frank Lloyd Wright, no matter if his message was too Middle Western to be taken very seriously in this corner of the East.

Nor is this a book in which buildings are treated merely as subjects, to be dissected by architectural students proving their knowledge of the craft. Any building stands for the hopes or fears of a generation: *why* buildings were built in such a way at such a time is just as fascinating a topic as the study of plans and elevations. There is only one plan and one elevation in this book. By way of recompense there is a good deal of information about what manner of men the clients were. They paid the bills. They deserve our respect, just as do the architects.

Finally, although no claim is made that here is a book without an error of fact or mistake in judgment, this is a book by one who has done his best to see the evidence with his own eyes. Of the 230 photographs, all but ten are the work of the author, and only three of the ten are of buildings still standing. As no photographer needs to be told, photographs are no substitute for giving a good look yourself at the thing you are talking about.

At best, photographs are invitations to go and see for yourself. Which is what the author hopes will happen.

1

I

The Dust of Dead Saints, or

THE SEVENTEENTH CENTURY

IF THE DUST OF DEAD SAINTS could give us any protection, we are not without it," declared Cotton Mather, the minister at 22 of Boston's North Church. His *Magnalia Christi Americana*, one of the 382 books he published in his industrious career, describes *"the wonders of the Christian religion, flying from the depravations of Europe to the American strand."* It is an earnest book, revealing the earnestness of the settlers of the seventeenth century. "I mourn exceedingly," he confessed, "and *I fear, I fear*, the sins of New England will ere long be read in its punishments." He added: "I have known it sometimes remark'd that very notorious and resolved sleepers at sermons often have some remarkable suddenness in the circumstances of their death."

Mather's fellow Congregationalist Judge Samuel Sewall, who graduated from Harvard College just seven years ahead of Mather, may be admired for the courage with which he admitted his mistake in sentencing the witches of Salem. Yet his temperament, like Mather's, was not exactly jovial. "We bury our little daughter," runs the famous entry in his diary for December 25, 1696. "I went at noon to see in what order things were set, and there I was entertained with a view of, and converse with, the Coffins of my dear Father Hull, Mother Hull, Cousin Quinsey, and my Six Children . . . 'Twas an awful, yet pleasing Treat; Having said, the Lord knows who shall be brought hether [*sic*] next, I came away."

It would be idle to look for architecture as a fine art in the New England that men like Mather and Sewall dominated, even though the Reverend John Wise, writing in 1721, or barely 20 years after the

Magnalia went to the printers, had a kind word for the things of this world. Wise, who enjoyed the sight of fine coaches and chariots, hoped for the day when a certain degree of luxury would be excused. He wanted, he said, "a Generous People, that would banish sordidness, and live Bright and Civil, with fine Accomplishments about them."

As we now know, the settlers of seventeenth-century New England erected no log cabins: these were introduced by the Swedes descending the Delaware. The little comfort of the Puritans was most precarious. "After they have thus found out a place of aboad," wrote Edward Johnson in his *Wonder-working Providence*, "they burrow themselves in the Earth for their first shelter under some Hill-side, casting the Earth aloft upon Timber, they make a smoaky fire against the Earth at the highest side, and thus these poor servants of Christ provide shelter for themselves, their Wives and little ones, keeping off the short showers from their Lodgings, but the long raines penetrate through . . . yet in these poor Wigwames [*sic*] they sing Psalmes, pray and praise their God, till they can provide them houses."

Providing houses took some time. However, Johnson concludes that "the Lord hath been pleased to turn all the wigwams, huts and hovels the English dwelt in at their first coming, into orderly, fair and well-built houses, well-furnished many of them, together with Orchards filled with goodly fruit trees and gardens with variety of flowers."

The weather-boarded frame houses that have survived tell of the devotion of the carpenters to the tradition of the southeastern counties of England, particularly that of Essex, where such houses were most frequent. The walls might be filled with wattle-and-daub, or occasionally bricks. Then the clapboards could be fastened to the studs with hand-forged nails. What purpose was served by the overhanging second story, or "jetty," is unknown, but it did provide the excuse for the pendants to be found at the Parson Capen house in Topsfield, Massachusetts. As for the floor plans, it has been argued that the typical seventeenth-century house was *not* built room-from-room, from a single-room end-chimney plan to a two-room plan with central chimney, plus a lean-to. The theory has been advanced that every house, small or large, was modeled after a house-type in Old England, and was full-grown the day the family moved in.

Since the Old Ship Meeting-House at Hingham, Massachusetts is the only church in New England dating from the seventeenth century, it has been studied with the greatest care by Hugh Morrison and other architectural historians, who have tried to imagine all the sacrifices to which the tried and true Congregationalists submitted. The altar was omitted, which may have been a relief, and it may have been an inspiration to gaze up at the pulpit at the middle of the long side of the rectangle. The benches, however, were no joy: men and women sat at opposite ends of the room, with nothing but a single timber to support their shoulder blades. Yet the building at Hingham, originally measuring 45 by 55 feet and costing £430, was paid for by the direct taxation of the 143 members of the congregation.

Such details are of considerable interest to the antiquarians of the twentieth century who often forget that there was a time when our colonial architecture was considered reprehensible. A Mrs. L. C. Tuthill, who in 1848 published the first American history of architecture, was delighted to point out that our colonial buildings were, happily, "all of such perishable materials that they will not much longer remain to annoy travelers in *search of the picturesque* through the beautiful villages of New England."

The revival of interest in colonial architecture did not begin until 1869 when Richard Upjohn, who earned his own reputation as a master of the Gothic Revival, dared to say a kind word at an architects' convention. "May we not gain a valuable lesson while contemplating these works of our forefathers?" he asked. "Old and quaint as they are, will we not see by comparing them with the works of our own hands that their authors regarded the law of harmony between a building and its surroundings better than we do at the present day?" Upjohn's advice was taken seriously by Stanford White and Charles Follen McKim, who made their famous walking and sketching trip up the New England coast in 1877, one result of which was to launch the Colonial Revival.

Residence of Jonathan Fayerbanke (Fairbanks house), Dedham, Massachusetts, c. 1636. Open. Fairbanks Family Association.

5

Above: Residence of Reverend Joseph Capen, Topsfield, Massachusetts, c. 1683. Open. Topsfield Historical Society. *Opposite:* Hearth in Capen house.

7

Old Ship Meeting-House, Hingham, Massachusetts, c. 1681. Widened 1731 and 1755. Restored 1930.

Residence of Benjamin Abbott, Andover, Massachusetts, c. 1685. Abbott was one of those who accused "Goody" Martha Carrier, hanged as a witch on August 19, 1692.

9

Opposite, top: Residence of Joseph Clay, Guilford, Connecticut, c. 1670. *Bottom:* Residence of Abraham Hoxie, Sandwich, Massachusetts, c. 1637? This 1959 restoration of a typical Cape Cod saltbox has been opened by the town of Sandwich. *Above:* Residence of John Turner (House of Seven Gables), Salem, Massachusetts, c. 1668. This site of Hawthorne's novel has been opened by the House of Seven Gables Settlement Association.

II

The Episcopalians Slyly Got into It, or

THE EIGHTEENTH CENTURY

THE SPIRIT OF COMMERCE, Madam," John Adams was telling his friend Mercy Warren in 1776, "which even insinuates itself into families, and influences Holy Matrimony, and thereby corrupts the morals of families as well as destroys their happiness . . . is incompatible with that purity of heart and greatness of soul which is so necessary for an happy republic."

For once Adams was wrong: a republic which scorns the profit motive does not deserve to exist. Moreover, the piling up of profits in the eighteenth century enabled the New England colonists to indulge in their own Georgian version of Renaissance architecture. But for men like the Rhode Island privateer Simeon Potter who cried: *Make money! Make money! I would plow the ocean into pea porridge to make money!* no further advance could have been made in the direction of splendor. Potter was an inspiration to any ambitious craftsman. So was Governor John Wentworth of New Hampshire, nephew and heir of the Benning Wentworth who accumulated something like 100,000 acres of timber-producing land in the 25 years in which he was Governor. And so was Thomas Hancock of Boston, who built his fortune out of dealing not only in Bibles and whalebone but army contracts as well.

Peter Harrison was certainly no stranger to the profit motive. This Quaker from York in Old England, who got to Newport, Rhode Island in 1739, when 23, became our first architect. That is, he was the first to design buildings for others to erect. Too shrewd to think of depending on his drafting board for a livelihood, he earned a good living at Newport out of trading with the Manigaults of South Carolina.

By the time he died of a heart attack in the spring of 1775, he was envisaging a comfortable old age as Collector of Customs at New Haven, Connecticut.

Harrison's rise in the world was rapid, so rapid that he must always have had an eye for the main chance. While still an employee in the Newport counting house of John Banister, he got Elizabeth Pelham with child. He then married her and the £20,000 sterling she had in her own name. Nor was he a Quaker for long. As early as 1745 he made his peace with the Church of England, becoming a member of Trinity Parish, Newport.

As an Episcopalian, Harrison moved in a world that the steadfast Congregationalist Ezra Stiles regarded with some suspicion. In 1748 Harrison (or rather his brother who represented him in his absence in England) was awarded the contract for the library which the merchant Abraham Redwood, Jr. presented the town. "This set out as a Quaker affair," murmured Stiles. "Through the blindness of Mr. Redwood . . . the Episcopalians slyly got into it and obtained a majority which they are careful to keep."

Harrison's biographer Carl Bridenbaugh has told us that the façade of the library, rusticated wood in imitation of dressed stone, could have been based on a design found in two books in the architect's library — either Hoppus's *Palladio* or Ware's *Designs of Inigo Jones and others*. But Harrison was most ingenious in adapting English Palladianism for American use and honestly deserved this handsome commission.

From that day on he was not forgotten. He is said to have planned Redwood's summer house, now moved to the library grounds. And in 1759 he was asked by the Sephardic Jews of Congregation Jeshuat Israel to create the synagogue over which Rabbi Isaac Touro, then lately arrived from the Rabbinical Academy in Amsterdam, presided. By 1761 Harrison was sketching yet another Newport monument, the Market House on Long Wharf. He was also to be the architect of Christ Church, Cambridge, and King's Chapel in Boston, whose challenge could be compared to that of the library and the synagogue.

We may never know who contrived the elegance of Jeremiah Lee's mansion in Marblehead, or who worried over the details of the Moffat-Ladd house in Portsmouth, but the ambition of prosperous New Englanders could not be denied. The architect who followed most cleverly in the Palladian tradition of Harrison was William Sprats, who after fighting with the Royal Artillery in the American Revolution refused to return to England. Instead he endowed the villages of Litchfield and Farmington with the most distinguished town houses of eighteenth-century Connecticut.

It was fortunate that John Adams, who could argue so convincingly when it came to politics, found so few to listen to him on the subject of architecture. "Is it possible," he asked a friend as late as 1817, "to enlist the Fine Arts on the side of Truth, of Virtue, of Piety, or even of Honor? From the dawn of History they have been prostituted to the Service of Superstition and Despotism. . . . It is vain to think of restraining the Fine Arts. Luxury will follow riches, and the Fine Arts luxury, in spite of all that wisdom can do."

RICHARD MUNDAY, Old Colony House, Newport, Rhode Island, 1739. Governor John Wanton headed the committee that hired master carpenter Munday to build this seat of government, turned into a barracks by the British during the Revolution, and later made into a hospital for the French troops. Washington dined in its great hall when he visited our French allies. Open. Old Colony House Association.

Above: RICHARD MUNDAY, interior, Trinity Church, Newport, Rhode Island, 1725. One of Wren's London churches could have inspired this Anglican house of worship. The organ, signed by Robert Bridges of London, and dated 1733, was the gift of George Berkeley, the future Bishop of Cloyne, who spent two years at Newport when his projected college for Negroes in Bermuda failed to materialize. With Berkeley came John Smibert, America's first professional painter. *Opposite:* Residence of Jonathan Nichols (Hunter House), Newport, Rhode Island, 1748. Built for the Deputy Governor of the colony, this handsome gambrel-roofed house was later the home of two governors and an ambassador to Brazil. Opened, with its superlative collection of Townsend and Goddard furniture, by the Preservation Society of Newport County.

Above: PETER HARRISON, Market House, Newport, Rhode Island, 1761. Open. Carl Bridenbaugh has suggested that Harrison may have depended in this instance on an engraving of Old Somerset House in Colin Campbell's *Vitruvius Britannicus. Opposite:* PETER HARRISON, Touro Synagogue, Newport, Rhode Island, 1759-63. Exterior and interior. Open since 1946 as a national historic site. "It is now no more that toleration is spoken of, as if it was by the indulgence of one class of people, that another enjoyed the exercise of their inherent natural rights," George Washington addressed Congregation Jeshuat Israel on August 17, 1790. "For happily the Government of the United States, which gives to bigotry no sanction, to persecution no assistance, requires only that they who live under its protection should demean themselves as good citizens, in giving it on all occasions their effectual support." When the Congregation built this temple, Rabbi Isaac Touro could have taught Harrison the layout of a Spanish-Portuguese synagogue. That of Amsterdam could have been seen by the architect on his visit to the Low Countries in 1744. Kent's *Designs of Inigo Jones* seems to have influenced the interior; the ark may have been based on a design for a Tuscan altarpiece found in Batty Langley's *Treasury of Designs.*

Above: PETER HARRISON, Redwood Library, Newport, Rhode Island, 1748. The statue of Washington by Houdon is a replica of the original in the capitol at Richmond, Virginia. *Below:* Summer House for Abraham Redwood, c. 1743. This rusticated octagonal building could have been inspired by Plate LXXX of James Gibbs' *Book of Architecture,* 1728. *Opposite:* PETER HARRISON, Christ Church, Cambridge, Massachusetts, 1760-61. Exterior and interior. Carl Bridenbaugh thinks the models for the Ionic columns in the interior may have come from James Gibb's *Rules for Drawing.*

PETER HARRISON, King's Chapel, Boston, Massachusetts, 1749-58. Exterior and interior. The steeple that Harrison planned was never to be built. Originally an Anglican church, it was later taken over by the Unitarians. Although Harrison drew once again on Batty Langley's *Treasury* and Gibbs' *Rules,* he was expressing himself with a certain freedom.

Above: Residence of Joseph Atwood, Chatham, Massachusetts, 1752. This stubborn gambrel-roofed house, built by a shipmaster and later lived in by the novelist Joseph C. Lincoln, tells of a New England that had not the slightest interest in elegance. Open. Chatham Historical Society. *Below:* Doorway. Residence of Eleazer Porter, Hadley, Massachusetts, c. 1757. Here is a broken pediment of the kind that was so popular in the Connecticut Valley.

Left: WILLIAM PRICE, Old North Church, Boston, Massachusetts, 1723. Price was a Boston print-seller who is said to have made a study of Wren's London churches before planning Old North (or Christ Church) for the Anglicans. Old North is identified with Paul Revere's famous ride. From the upper window of the belfry chamber sexton Robert Newman flashed the two lanterns that were seen by a man on horesback on the shore at Charlestown. Bulfinch was later to supply the steeple here seen, later lost in the 1938 hurricane. *Photo Samuel Chamberlain. Right:* ROBERT TWELVES, Old South Church, Boston, Massachusetts, 1729-30. Old North's design had its influence on this Congregationalist church, where the protest was held that led to the Boston Tea Party. *Photo Samuel Chamberlain.*

Above: Old State House, Boston, Massachusetts, 1748. Restored 1882, but according to a remodeling of 1830. *Opposite, top:* Residence of Thomas Hancock, Boston, Massachusetts, 1737-40. Pulled down in 1863, this residence on Beacon Hill inspired the replica on the grounds of the New York State Historical Association at Ticonderoga, New York. Joshua Blanchard was the master mason on whom Hancock depended. "My gardens all lye on the south side of a hill with the most beautiful Assent to the top & its allowed on all hands the Kingdom of England don't afford so Fine a Prospect as I have both of land & water," Hancock was writing the London seedsman James Glen before the house was built. "Neither do I intend to Spare any Cost or pains in making my Gardens Beautifull or Profitable." In 1764 the house passed to Thomas Hancock's nephew John, the first signer of the Declaration of Independence. *Courtesy Boston Athenaeum. Photograph retaken by George Cushing.*

Below: Residence of John Vassall, Cambridge, Massachusetts, 1759. First owned by a Tory major in the British Army, it was enlarged in the nineteenth century by Henry Wadsworth Longfellow. Open. Longfellow Memorial Trust.

This page: Residence of Jeremiah Lee, Marblehead, Massachusetts, 1768. Exterior and interior. This merchant and his wife were painted by John Singleton Copley. Open. Marblehead Historical Society. *Opposite, top:* Lady Pepperrell House, Kittery Point, Maine, 1760. Here lived the widow of Sir William Pepperrell who forced the surrender in 1745 of the French fortress at Louisburg, Nova Scotia. Open. Society for the Preservation of New England Antiquities. *Bottom:* Residence of John Sergeant, Stockbridge, Massachusetts, 1739. Sergeant, the first missionary to the Housatonic Indians, was the first occupant of this severe house whose only ornamentation is the broken "Connecticut Valley" pediment above the door. Open. Trustees of Reservations.

Above: Residence of Captain Archibald McPhedris (McPhedris-Warner house), Portsmouth, New Hampshire, 1718-23. McPhedris was a fur trader so successful that he not only joined the Governor's Council but married the daughter of Governor John Wentworth. Their daughter, who married Jonathan Warner, later occupied the house, which must have been visited by the Reverend Arthur Browne in charge of Portsmouth's Queen's Chapel. Browne was an Anglican who had no use for the enthusiasm of John Wesley's friend George Whitefield. "My small flock (Blessed be God!) have almost escaped the infection," Browne reported in 1742 after Whitefield descended on the

town. "Three or four only have fallen away, but the loss is not much to be regretted, as they were persons of no *extraordinary Reputation.* . . ." Open. Warner House Association. *This page:* Residence of Thomas Wentworth (Wentworth-Gardner house), Portsmouth, New Hampshire, 1760. This small but rather elegant house was presented to Thomas Wentworth by his mother Mrs. Mark Hunking Wentworth, whose husband got rich supplying the Royal Navy with masts and spars. Open. Wentworth-Gardner and Tobias Lear Houses Association.

Residence of Captain John Moffatt (Moffatt-Ladd house), Portsmouth, New Hampshire, 1763. Exterior and interior. This, the most imposing house of the eighteenth century on the New England seacoast, was built by Captain Moffatt (perhaps as a wedding gift) for his son Samuel, who had to flee to the West Indies from his creditors in 1768. In

1807 the house passed into the hands of Alexander Ladd. Open. Colonial Dames. The scenic wallpaper — *Vues d'Italie* by Joseph Dufour of Paris — dates from the early nineteenth century.

31

Dining room and hall window, Moffatt-Ladd house, Portsmouth, New Hampshire.

Above: Trinity Church, Brooklyn, Connecticut, 1771. This Anglican church, which looks so like a meeting-house, was donated by Godfrey Malbone, a Tory from Newport, Rhode Island. *Below:* Meeting-house, Sandown, New Hampshire, 1774. In its stark simplicity this is one of the best examples extant of the type.

Opposite, top: Dartmouth Hall, Hanover, New Hampshire, 1784-91. Burned in 1904, this building (originally a frame structure) was rebuilt in brick. There was another rebuilding, this time of the interior, after a fire in 1935. *Bottom:* Connecticut Hall, Yale University, New Haven, Connecticut, 1750-52. In the eighteenth century the progress of Yale College was watched with misgivings by many of the best people in New York. "It is my desire," wrote Lewis Morris, Jr. of the Manor of Morrisania in his will, "that my son Gouverneur Morris may have the best education that is to be had in Europe or America, but my express will and directions are that he never be sent for that purpose to the Colony of Connecticut lest he should imbibe in his youth that low craft and cunning so incident to the people of that country, which is so interwoven in their constitution that all their art cannot disguise it from the world, though many of them under the sanctified garb of religion have endeavored to impose themselves on the world as honest men." *Above:* Residence of Joseph Webb, Wethersfield, Connecticut, 1752. In the council room of this house Washington and Rochambeau are said to have planned the Yorktown campaign in 1781. General Samuel B. Webb (Joseph's son) was on Washington's staff. Open. Colonial Dames.

Above: WILLIAM SPRATS, residence of Uriah Tracy, Litchfield, Connecticut, 1790. Originally Sheldon's Tavern, dating from 1760, this was remodeled by Sprats to suit Senator Uriah Tracy, who grew to be so extreme a Federalist that he joined Timothy Pickering of Massachusetts at the Hartford Convention to consider New England's secession from the Union. *Opposite:* WILLIAM SPRATS,

"The Lindens," residence of Julius Deming, Litchfield, Connecticut, 1790-93. One of the more important of Sprats's commissions, "The Lindens" was built for the local merchant who bought into the ship *Trident* and helped found the Litchfield China Trading Company.

Above and opposite: WILLIAM SPRATS, residence of Samuel Cowles, Farmington, Connecticut, 1780. The Cowleses were merchant adventurers who traded mainly with the West Indies.

III

Mr. Bulfinch's Misadventures:

THE FEDERAL ERA: 1789-1830

HIS MOTHER WAS AN APTHORP, and when he married, he married an Apthorp. From which anyone might have guessed that Charles Bulfinch would enjoy to the fullest the prosperity that came to Boston when her seamen began to circle the globe. However, this was not to be. Although Bulfinch was one of the shareholders in the *Columbia* — the first American ship to go around the world, earning her a thirteen-gun salute on entering Boston harbor on August 9, 1790 at the end of her three-year voyage — he was no businessman and went bankrupt not once but twice.

We may regret this. And we may regret the fact that he spent the month of July, 1811, in jail for debt. But if it had not been for Bulfinch's misadventures he might have remained all his life an amateur architect. He became a professional because he was hard-pressed.

Graduating from Harvard with the class of 1781, he spent some time in the counting house of Joseph Barrell. "I was," he reported, "at leisure to cultivate a taste for architecture, which was encouraged by attending to Mr. Barrell's improvement of his estate and the [improvements] on our dwelling house and the houses of some friends, all of which had become extremely dilapidated during the war."

By the summer of 1785 he was off for a Grand Tour of a year and a half. He got to know London, Florence, Parma, and Milan and in Paris our Minister Thomas Jefferson showed him around. "I was delighted," Bulfinch recorded, "in observing the numerous objects and beauties of nature and art that I met with on all sides, particularly the wonders of

architecture and the kindred arts of painting and sculpture . . . but these pursuits did not confirm me in any business habits of buying and selling, on the contrary they had a powerful adverse influence on my whole after life."

On his return to Boston he could not settle down, even after becoming the husband of Hannah Apthorp in the fall of 1788. "I was," he said, "warmly received by friends, and passed a season of leisure, pursuing no business, but giving gratuitous advice in architecture, and looking forward to an establishment in life."

Disaster struck when he began speculating in real estate in 1793, building Tontine Crescent in the South End of Boston between Milk and Summer Streets. These connected brick houses, so graceful that they could easily be compared to Robert Adam's Charlotte Square in Edinburgh, erected two years before this, brought about his ruin. 1793 was a depression year and the houses were difficult to unload, despite the fine urn he brought back from the continent to decorate Franklin Place, as the north end of the development was named. By 1796 he went into bankruptcy.

In 1799, such was his standing in the community, he was re-elected a Selectman, and was Chairman of the Board for the next nineteen years. This was an unpaid office. To make ends meet, he had himself made Superintendent of Police which paid him $600 a year and ultimately $1,000. He had, it seems, no understanding of the business side of architecture. When a granddaughter ventured to ask whether another member of the family should turn architect, he vetoed the notion. "The states and prominent towns," he argued in his old age, "were already supplied with their chief buildings, and he hardly thought a young man could make a living as an architect."

His second misadventure occurred when he tried his luck with certain mud flats along the Charles. These had been considered worthless in 1799, and so were left in his possession at the time. He began filling in these flats, with the idea of extending Charles Street to the West Boston Bridge, just when the Embargo killed all hope of breaking even. "The company of Otis & Company," he wrote, referring to the high-living Federalist politico Harrison Gray Otis, "men of large capital, were able to wait for better times for the sale of their lands, from which they have since realized immense profit, but no sales could then be made by me, and demands were pressing with accumulating interest, so that I was obliged once more to surrender all property, and was even more reduced than before, and we were obliged to leave our neat and commodious home for a humbler and inferior one."

The Tontine Crescent has vanished, and so has the mansion he designed in 1792 for Joseph Barrell. This exhibited a splendid oval drawing room, proving that Bulfinch was abreast of the innovations in planning that were then (thanks to the presence of several French architects, refugees from the Revolution) beginning to be introduced to the United States. It would be delightful to assign to Bulfinch "Gore Place," the mansion of Governor Christopher Gore at Waltham, since it is the most advanced house still standing of the Federal period, but there is as yet no evidence that he contrived that oval drawing room and eliptical sitting room.

However, what is left of Bulfinch is sufficient to ensure his reputation. There is the State House in Boston, where he recalled the splendors of Sir William Chambers' Somerset House in London. There is the Church of Christ in Lancaster, which must be considered one of the greater American churches of this era. And aside from his work for Harvard College and Phillips Academy, there are the three notable houses he fashioned for Harrison Gray Otis in Boston. Otis — who grew richer and richer after joining the Mount Vernon Proprietors who bought up most of Beacon Hill for a most profitable speculation — was not the man to think of relieving an architect in distress. More important to Otis was the splendid Lowestoft punch bowl in his front hall.

Samuel McIntire, Bulfinch's contemporary in Salem, was not half so inventive — he was not one to think of any innovations in the plans of his solid square mansions — but to him must go the credit for the architectural reputation of the seaport that was for a time a world center for the pepper trade.

A more significant figure than McIntire was Asher Benjamin, the carpenter from Greenfield, Massachusetts, who had the modesty to recognize that Bulfinch was the "first architect of New England." In 1797 Benjamin brought out *The Country Builder's Assistant*, the very first handbook to be published by an American. It was certainly an inspiration to Lavius Fillmore who in 1806 modeled the extraordinary First Church in Bennington, Vermont, after one of Benjamin's illustrations. By that time the Congregationalists had abandoned the meeting-house plan to which they had held so long for something that could have passed for an Anglican house of worship.

But even the most superficial glance at the architecture of the Federal period would have to acknowledge the talent of Joseph Brown of Providence. This member of the famous trading family, who eventually taught philosophy at the College of Rhode Island (as Brown University was then called), was an amateur architect of such distinction that he and his imitators made the hill above Providence quite as commanding as the streets of Salem.

CHARLES BULFINCH, residence of Harrison Gray Otis (Number One), 141 Cambridge Street, Boston, Massachusetts, 1795-96. Exterior and two interiors. This was restored in 1916 to serve as the headquarters of the Society for the Preservation of New England Antiquities. Recent restorations of the interior have been under the direction of Abbott Lowell Cummings. The semicircular porch is the only item on the exterior which does not jibe with Bulfinch's own elevation. The pastels (by an anonymous artist) are of Deacon Sharp and his wife Hepzibah. Open.

42

Above: CHARLES BULFINCH, Central Pavilion, Tontine Crescent, Boston, Massachusetts, 1793-94. *Courtesy Boston Athenaeum. Photograph retaken by George Cushing.* Demolished c. 1858. *Opposite, top:* CHARLES BULFINCH, residence of Harrison Gray Otis (Number Three), 45 Beacon Street, Boston, Massachusetts, 1805-1808. Mayor Philip Hone of New York, who knew a thing or two about high life, declared that Otis was "the most perfect gentleman of my acquaintance." And John Quincy Adams confessed that "it has not fallen to my lot to meet a man more skilled in the useful art of entertaining his friends than Otis; and among the many admirable talents that he possesses, there is none that I should have been more frequently and more strangely promoted to envy; if the natural turn of my disposition had been envious." *Bottom:* CHARLES BULFINCH, residence of Harrison Gray Otis (Number Two), 85 Mount Vernon Street, Boston, Massachusetts, 1800-02.

44

Opposite: CHARLES BULFINCH, Church of Christ, Lancaster, Massachusetts, 1816. (Also shown as frontispiece.) Exterior and interior. The master builder, Thomas Hearsey of Lancaster, added the volutes to the tower and raised the three arches of the entrance to the same height, omitting the swag panels Bulfinch had devised above the arch to the left and that to the right. *Above:* CHARLES BULFINCH, south front of Massachusetts State House, Boston, Massachusetts, 1795-96. "It is in the style of a building celebrated all over Europe," wrote Bulfinch of his plans to the legislative committee. He was referring to his model, Somerset House in London, begun by Sir William Chambers in 1778. Additions were made to the north front in 1831 by Isaiah Rogers and in 1853-56 by Gridley J. F. Bryant; these were totally obscured by an extension made from 1889 to 1895 that was six times the size of the original building. Between 1914 and 1917 marble and granite wings by William Chapman, R. Clipston Sturgis and Robert D. Andrews enclosed Bulfinch's work to the north.

47

Above: Charles Bulfinch, Connecticut State House, Hartford, Connecticut, 1793-96. This was turned into a city hall upon the completion of Richard Michell Upjohn's new state house in 1879, and in 1918-21 was restored by Robert D. Andrews of Boston and H. Hilliard Smith of Hartford. *Opposite:* Charles Bulfinch, Faneuil Hall, Boston, Massachusetts, 1805-06. This building was originally the design of John Smibert, the painter who accompanied George Berkeley to Newport. Smibert's work of 1740-42 was much altered by Bulfinch, who doubled the width, added a third story and set the cupola on the Dock Street end. In 1898-99 the structure was entirely rebuilt; with the exception of the old cherry rail on the stairs, all wood and combustible material was replaced by iron, steel and stone. Bulfinch might not have been called in if the inadequacy of Faneuil Hall for town meetings had not been obvious: in the Smibert design the assembly room above the market arcade could hold no more than a thousand people. Open.

Below: CHARLES BULFINCH, Massachusetts General Hospital, Boston, Massachusetts, 1818-23. The pediment of this south front has been somewhat altered, and the wings doubled in length. This was Bulfinch's last Boston commission. "I confess that it gratifies me," he wrote, "but more on my children's account than my own. They will feel pleasure that my last act for Boston is accepted under circumstances which preclude the possibility of personal influence." Plate 15 in John Soane's *Designs in Architecture* has been suggested by the Bulfinch scholar Harold Kirker as a possible source. *Opposite:* CHARLES BULFINCH, University Hall, Harvard College, Cambridge, Massachusetts, 1813-14. The cupola that Bulfinch contemplated was never built, and the building was somewhat altered in 1842.

Above: CHARLES BULFINCH, Bulfinch Hall, Phillips Academy, Andover, Massachusetts, 1818-19. This was restored in 1936-37. *Opposite:* CHARLES BULFINCH, Pearson Hall, Phillips Academy, Andover, Massachusetts, 1817-18. Named after the first principal of the academy, this was originally Bartlet Chapel, built by determined Congregationalists for their seminary. In 1924, sixteen years after the seminary moved to Newton, this building was taken over by the Academy and the interior much altered.

Above: "Gore Place," Waltham, Massachusetts, 1797-1804. This country estate of Governor Christopher Gore, with its oval drawing room and eliptical sitting room, must have been planned by someone familiar with the generous innovations of eighteenth-century French architecture. Tauzia, the château designed in 1778 by Victor Louis at Gradignan near Bordeaux, presents an interesting parallel. Open. Gore Place Association. *Opposite:* SAMUEL McINTIRE, residence of Jerathmiel Peirce (Peirce-Nichols house), Salem, Massachusetts, 1782. In 1801 Peirce asked McIntire to remodel the east parlor to celebrate his daughter Sally's marriage to George Nichols. Peirce, who made his money out of the East India trade, was rich, but not so rich as Elias Hasket Derby, who died in 1799 worth $1,500,000. McIntire's most splendid commission, that for Derby's town house, may be studied only in drawings: it was destroyed in 1815. The Peirce-Nichols house is open thanks to Essex Institute.

SAMUEL McINTIRE, residence of John Gardiner (Gardiner-White-Pingree house), Salem, Massachusetts, 1804-05. Exterior and two interiors. Open. Essex Institute. The Salem clergyman William Bentley may have been thinking of the choice interiors of this sea captain's house when he saluted McIntire on his death in 1811. Wrote diarist Bentley: "This day Salem was deprived of one of the most ingenious men it had in it, Samuel McIntire, aet. 54, in Summer Street. He was descended of a family of carpenters who had no claims on public favor and was educated at a branch of that business. By attention he soon gained a superiority to all of his occupation and the present Court House, the North and South meeting houses, and indeed all the improvements of Salem for nearly thirty years past have been done under his eye. In sculpture he had no rival in New England and I possess some specimens which I should not scruple to compare with any I ever saw. . . . He had a fine person, a majestic appearance, calm countenance, great self-command and amiable temper. He was welcome but never intruded." The bust of Ann Maria Pingree (Mrs. Stephen Goodhue Wheatland) dates from 1877, and is the work of Preston Powers. Mrs. Wheatland's father was David Pingree, sixth Mayor of Salem. Above the mantel is the engraving *Liberty in the form of the Goddess of Youth giving support to the Bald Eagle*, the work of E. Savage, 1796.

Above: Asher Benjamin, Old West Church, Boston, Massachuetts, 1806. The church has been converted into a branch of the Boston Public Library. *Opposite:* Asher Benjamin, Old South Church, Windsor, Vermont, 1798.

LAVIUS FILLMORE, First Congregational Church, Bennington, Vermont, 1806. Exterior and interior. How deeply Fillmore depended on Benjamin for his inspiration is proved in the plate from Benjamin's first handbook on the following page.

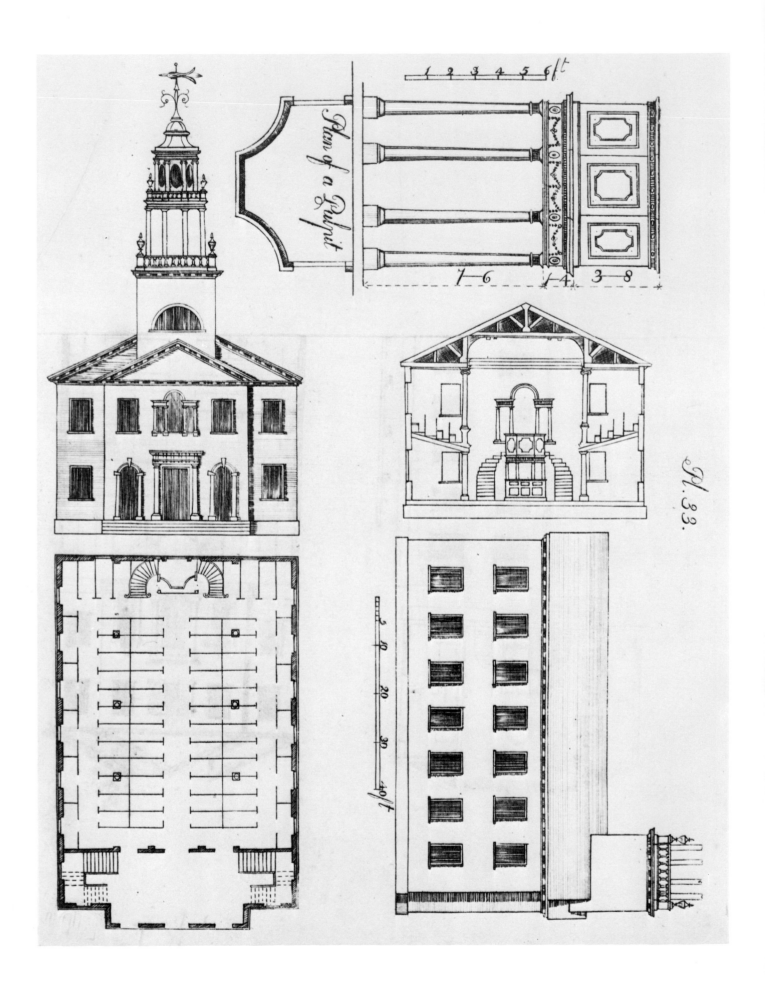

Plan of a Pulpit

Pl. 33.

Opposite: ASHER BENJAMIN, Plate 33 from *The Country Builder's Assistant,* Boston, 1797. *Photo: New-York Historical Society. Above:* LAVIUS FILLMORE, First Church, Middlebury, Vermont, 1809. Here again Fillmore was relying on Benjamin's plate.

Above: First Church, Templeton, Massachusetts, 1811. The unknown builder of this church was, like Fillmore, in debt to the high standards Benjamin was imposing. *Opposite:* WILLIAM RHODES, Round Church, Richmond, Vermont, 1813. Novelties were indulged in by carpenters who did not study their Benjamin.

Opposite, top: Residence of Job Lyman, Woodstock, Vermont, 1809. The portico of this house for Lyman, who was both lawyer and banker, was doubtlessly added at the beginning of the romantic decades. *Below:* Residence of Jonas Galusha, Shaftsbury Center, Vermont, c. 1807. Galusha was a prominent Baptist who served as Governor of Vermont. *Above:* JOSEPH BROWN, residence of John Brown, Providence, Rhode Island, 1786-88. Of the four Brown brothers, who traded staves, hoops and tobacco for molasses, building the great fortune of Rhode Island in the Federal era and founding the first cotton mills, Joseph was the amateur architect. In 1787 John Brown inaugurated the trade of Rhode Island with the East Indies by financing the *General Washington.* Open. Rhode Island Historical Society.

Opposite: JOSEPH BROWN, residence of Joseph Brown, Providence, Rhode Island, 1774.
Above: JOSEPH BROWN, University Hall, Brown University, Providence, Rhode Island, 1770.

Above: CALEB ORMSBEE, residence of Joseph Nightingale, Providence, Rhode Island, 1792. Nightingale was another prominent Providence merchant. *Opposite:* RUSSELL WARREN, "Linden Place," residence of George DeWolfe, Bristol, Rhode Island, 1810. The façade of this mansion for one of the trading families of Bristol has been somewhat altered.

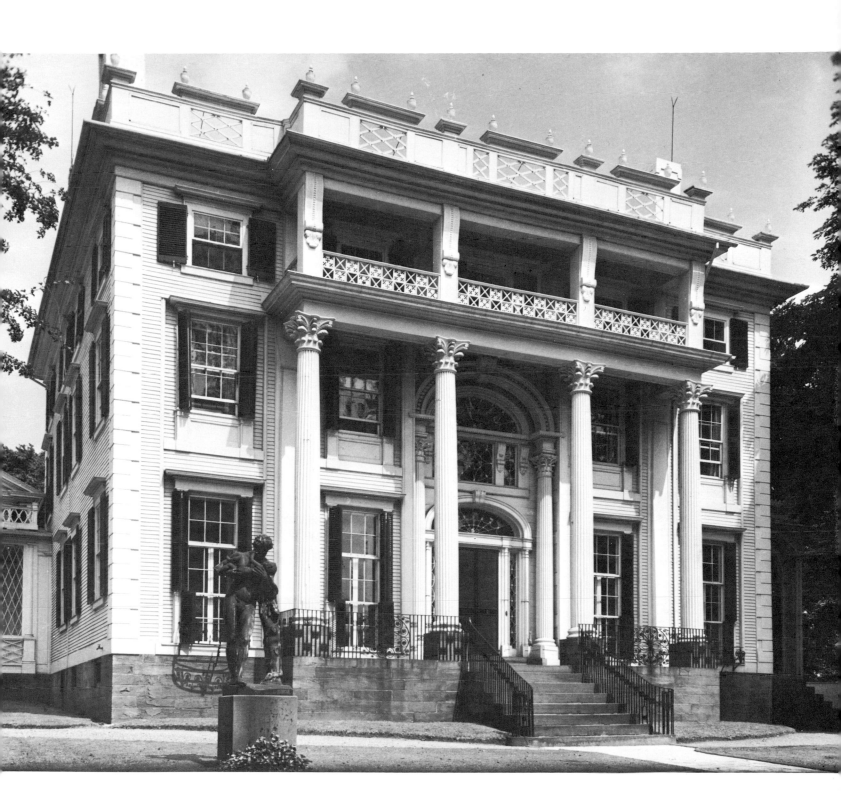

Opposite, top: House at 154 High Street, Bristol, Rhode Island, c. 1810. *Bottom:* Saint Paul's Church, Wickford, Rhode Island, 1707-1800. Restored in 1914, this church, which once stood on the road running west from Pender Zeke's Corner, was moved to this site in 1800. The broken pediment is obviously an addition of the late eighteenth century. *Above:* Residence of General John Wheeler, Orford, New Hampshire, c. 1820.

73

Opposite: Residence of Lord Timothy Dexter, Newburyport, Massachusetts, c. 1810. *Lithograph by B. W. Thayer courtesy Boston Athenaeum. Photo: George Cushing.* Dexter, the great eccentric of New England in the Federal era, began, about 1801, transforming the mansion of Patrick Tracy, dating from 1771, into an outdoor museum. The picket fence was turned into an arch of welcome and on the high arch before the front door stood statues of Washington, Adams and Jefferson. The house is still standing, although not in the splendid condition of 1810. One of Dexter's coups as a businessman was to export warming pans to the West Indies; the captain in charge of the cargo removed their lids, renamed them skimmers, and sold them at a profit. As an author Dexter is remembered for *A Pickel for the knowing ones; or, Plain Truth in a Homespun Dress.* This was a book minus punctuation and legend has it that in the second edition Dexter announced that his readers "may peper and salt it as they plese." Unfortunately, no such note has been found in any copy of the second edition. With his house and grounds Dexter was eminently satisfied: "Steady men sayeth it is the first that it is the best in this Countery and other Countreys." *Below:* Residence of John Peirce, Portsmouth, New Hampshire, 1800.

Jack Tar   Kang Georg.   Lean Fred   General Washington   Law
    William Pitt   Lord Nelson   N. Bonaparte   in the West   J. Adams   T. Jefferson   T. Bradford   Gen Elliot   Louis XVI   the greatest Philosopher   Caleb Strong
    T. Bester   of the Western World

B. Franklin   Law   Law   Cromwell   Law   Marshall   Law   Sentinel

... character are Engraved on the Fascia of the Entablature of the Columns which being too small here to be made legible we place Respectively to their respective Statues

... of the Mansion of the late LORD TIMOTHY DEXTER, *in High Street, Newburyport, 1810.*

... faithfully delineated in order to convey a full representation of one of the whims of that most truly eccentric character whose many singularities of conduct, and speculations by which he acquired from the smallest beginnings a splendid fortune, are to be found
... the account of his Life. Written by Samuel L. Knapp Esq. & Published at Newburyport by James Lima, Boston, by John G. Tilton & Co. 324 Washington Street.

David Hoadley, United Church, New Haven, Connecticut, 1812-15. Hoadley was the leading architect of New Haven before Ithiel Town began his career.

Above: Residence of Ptolemy Edson, Chester Depot, Vermont, 1833. In Chester Depot, as in other parts of New England the Federal style lingered on long after the Gothic and the Greek Revival had become popular. Southern Windsor County has justly been called the stone-house belt of New England. Experts in putting the stone from Mount Flamstead and Mount Trebo to good use were the brothers Zephaniah and David Ordway. David was the curious mason who asked the pastor of the Universalist Church at Ludlow to preach his funeral sermon three years before he died. Writes Leon S.

Gay in *Vermont Life:* "Ordway was present and listened with great attention." *Opposite, top:* Residence of William Nichols (Nichols-Sortwell house), Wiscasset, Maine, 1807-08. This was turned into a hostelry before being restored by the Sortwell family. *Bottom:* Aaron Sherman, residence of Judge Thomas Ruggles, Columbia Falls, Maine, 1818. One of the best examples of the pride of Maine in the Federal era is this lumber dealer's mansion not far from the Canadian border. Open. Ruggles House Association.

IV

Gothic Gloom in Hartford:

THE ROMANTIC DECADES: 1830-1860

THERE IS NO BETTER GUIDE to follow down the romantic years in New England than Daniel Wadsworth of Hartford. Here was a connoisseur who could not help moving ahead of the times. In 1827, when Thomas Cole was only 26 and had yet to build his reputation as the leader of the Hudson River school of painting, he knew that he could dispose of his landscapes to the master of "Montevideo." This was the Gothic cottage that Wadsworth built for himself about 1818 at Avon on the outskirts of Hartford. A good dozen years would pass before the Gothic Revival began to sweep the nation. When it did, Wadsworth was pleased, so pleased that he took the trouble to lecture a young ladies' seminary on the beauties of pointed arches.

Gloom, Wadsworth admitted, was a desirable element in Gothic architecture, but it was not *inherent*. "There is," he preached to the young ladies, "nothing in the mere forms or embellishments of the pointed style of architecture in the least adapted to convey to the mind the impression of *Gothic gloom*. The proportions and decorations," he went on, "are light, graceful and elegant, and I have thought even when very young, and in Henry the Seventh's Chapel, which is one hundred feet in length, although awed by its gloom, that but for the rich twilight of its painted windows, and the dark color of its materials, rendered still more dark by time, all its forms, and all its proportions were entirely appropriate to a splendid banqueting room, and it then appeared to me that the different impressions, even in Westminster Abbey, into which this chapel opens, were caused wholly by the artificial

darkness, occasioned by shrouded windows, the gloomy color of the stone and deeper colored oak, its venerable age, the vast extent of the buildings, and the countless monuments which seem to crowd around you, as if the magnificent pile were raised only to shelter the great congregation of the dead, and as if the echo of each footstep were a voice of reproof to the living intruder."

Of course Wadsworth was not the first American to imagine how delightful the United States might be if remade in a medieval style. That honor belongs to Benjamin Henry Latrobe, chief architect of the Capitol in Washington, who in 1799 introduced both the Gothic and the Greek Revival to Philadelphia. But Wadsworth deserves to be remembered as one of the first to do battle for the Gothic cause, even though Andrew Jackson Downing, the landscape architect from Newburgh, New York was a crusader winning many more adherents with his handbooks for the American home. Downing cordially disliked the Greek Revival, which was more popular than he cared to confess. "The Greek temple disease has passed its crisis," he noted with considerable satisfaction in 1846. "The people have survived it."

The romantic revivals — aside from the Gothic and the Greek, there was a Moorish and even an Egyptian revival, not to mention the new Italian villa style — *may* be dismissed as simply an invitation to live in the world of make-believe: it is true that many a businessman was persuaded that by erecting a Gothic villa he could live in Gothic time once the day's work was done. But it is also true that each and every one of these revivals represented an attack on the supremacy of the Renaissance. The Renaissance had to be discredited if modern architecture were to make its appearance, and it is not surprising that Frank Lloyd Wright and nearly every other pioneer of the modern movement were tried and true Gothic men.

Daniel Wadsworth might have been surprised to learn that the Gothic Revival was revolutionary. He simply enjoyed it, as he did the capes of different colors that he wore, one on top of the other, as he walked the streets of Hartford. He was, we are told, "a fragile man with a stoop, fond of wearing even in the house an artist's cap and cloak, partly to protect himself from the drafts, of which he had an exaggerated dread, partly, we fancy, to exemplify in his person the artistic temperament."

No one ever accused his father, Jeremiah Wadsworth, the Commissary General of the American Army in the Revolution, of having an artistic temperament. In fact he was suspected of earning all too much money from his post. A good part of this inheritance was dedicated by his son to the founding in 1842 of Hartford's Wadsworth Atheneum. The museum, as you may have guessed, was Gothic, designed by Alexander Jackson Davis with his then partner Ithiel Town. It was quite understandable that Daniel Wadsworth selected Davis, for he enjoyed as an architect the same high reputation that came to Thomas Cole as a painter. Having done so much for his native city, the donor of the Atheneum must be excused for installing a foot stove in his pew at Center Church — a draft could easily upset his composure.

New England, it should be conceded, was not the center of American architecture in this period. New York City was in the thick of things, for that was where Alexander Jackson Davis had his office and where Richard Upjohn, the creator of Trinity Church on Broadway, nourished his ambition to build noble Anglican churches across the country. Philadelphia too was in the forefront: thanks to Nicholas Biddle of the Second Bank of the United States, the Girard College that Thomas U. Walter designed was, in Biddle's own words: "the most beautiful building now standing."

But New England was far from a backwater. It was visited by Davis, Upjohn and many other architects from New York. And its own architects were not to be disdained. There was Russell Warren, who gave Providence its arcade and Newport the elegant Greek Revival mansion of Levi Gale. There was Alexander Parris, the contriver of Saint Paul's Cathedral in Boston and the imposing Quincy Market. There was Isaiah Rogers, whose now vanished Tremont House in Boston established him as the foremost hotel designer in the country. There was Ammi B. Young, responsible for the eloquent Grecian capitol of Vermont. And finally there was Henry Austin of New Haven. After trying his hand at the Egyptian and the Gothic, he revealed he was a master of the Italian villa style in "Victoria Mansion" in Portland.

So much for architecture as a fine art in the romantic years. Architecture as building cannot be neglected, even though there is still much to learn about who designed the housing and the mills in towns like Lowell, Massachusetts and Manchester and Harrisville, New Hampshire. Finally, a tribute must be paid to the anonymous masons and contractors who built the granite monuments to commerce standing on the wharves of Boston. The simplicity of these structures must have haunted Henry Hobson Richardson when he meditated in the next generation over the plans for Boston's Trinity Church.

Above: DANIEL WADSWORTH, "Montevideo," residence of Daniel Wadsworth, Ave
Connecticut, c. 1818. One of the great admirers of "Montevideo," in all probability t
first Gothic Revival house in New England, was Professor Benjamin Silliman of Ya
who called on Wadsworth in 1819. Wrote Silliman: "Rocks and forests alone meet t
eye, and appear to separate you from all the rest of the world. But at the same mome
that you are contemplating this picture of the deepest solitude, you may, without lea
ing your place, merely by changing your position, see through one of the long Got
windows . . . the glowing western valley." The poetess Lydia Huntley Sigourney w
even more enthusiastic: *Pale envy's glance, the chill of fear, and war and discord co
not here,* she proclaimed. *Opposite, top:* TOWN & DAVIS, entrance, Wadsworth At
neum, Hartford, Connecticut, 1842. *Bottom:* TOWN & DAVIS, residence of Samuel R
sell, Middletown, Connecticut, 1828-30. This mansion of the China trader Russell h
been opened by Wesleyan University.

Opposite: A. J. Davis, residence of H. K. Harral, Bridgeport, Connecticut, 1846. Exterior and interior. Presented to the city of Bridgeport by the last owner Archer C. Wheeler, the Harral mansion was promptly demolished to make way for a parking lot. Harral was a leather dealer who came from Charleston, South Carolina. One of the ornaments of the Harral house was this statue of Pandora by Chauncy Ives. Davis was the most successful architect of his generation. He retired for all practical purposes from the profession in 1860, but was able to spend the last thirty-two years of his life in the quiet of his Gothic villa at Llewellyn Park, New Jersey.

Prison reform was the passion of his wife. His own head was stuffed with Gothic novels. He never stopped reading Mrs. Radcliffe and the others whom Jane Austen spoofed in *Northanger Abbey,* and very likely discussed this interesting topic with his friend Herman Melville on the walks they took together. *Above:* Joseph C. Wells, residence of H. C. Bowen, Woodstock, Connecticut, c. 1845. Bowen was the publisher of *The Independent* whose editor was Henry Ward Beecher. Architect Wells was also responsible for the Gothic First Presbyterian Church on Fifth Avenue, New York. Open. Society for the Preservation of New England Antiquities.

85

Below: LEOPOLD EIDLITZ, "Iranistan," residence of P. T. Barnum, Bridgeport, Connecticut, 1848. When architect Eidlitz called one day at "Iranistan," he was met at the front door by Barnum, who declared that his villa was the result of a "cosmopolitan competition" and cost $10,000. "No, it didn't," Eidlitz said. "Is your name Eidlitz?" asked Barnum, who knew that for once his bluff was called. This Moorish villa burned to the ground in 1857. *Photo of engraving courtesy The Connecticut Historical Society. Opposite, top:* HENRY AUSTIN, Grove Street Cemetery, New Haven, Connecticut, 1845-46. There were those who disapproved of the Egyptian Revival, especially when cemetery gates were in question. "Egyptian architecture," the *North American Review* argued in 1836, "reminds us of the religion which called it into being, the most degraded and revolting paganism which ever existed. It is the architecture of embalmed cats and deified crocodiles." *Bottom:* Residence of Richard Alsop IV, Middletown, Connecticut, 1836-40. Like the Samuel Russell residence, this Greek Revival villa has been opened by Wesleyan University.

THE DEAD SHALL BE RAISED.

Above: Lewis Wharf, Boston, Massachusetts, 1840. Although there is no evidence that H. H. Richardson strolled by the Boston wharves while a Harvard undergraduate, it seems likely that he appreciated the workmanship of the masons. *Opposite:* Boott Mills, Lowell, Massachusetts, c. 1850. Although the firm of Almy & Brown of Providence launched American cotton mills in 1791 by bringing over the Englishman Samuel Slater who reconstructed one of Richard Arkwright's spinning machines, this operation was dwarfed in 1822 when Nathan Appleton, Patrick Tracy Jackson and Kirk Boott established the Merrimack Manufacturing Company at Lowell. "From the beginning, Lowell had a high reputation for good order, morality, piety and all that was dear to the old-fashioned New Englander's heart," claimed Lucy Larcom, one of the mill hands who smuggled Bibles into the workrooms. "The overseer, caring more for the law than the gospel, confiscated all he found. He had his desk full of Bibles," she reported.

Above: Housing, Harrisville Manufacturing Co. (later the Cheshire Mills), Harrisville, New Hampshire, c. 1833. Asa Greenwood was the stonemason responsible for the charm of this mill town. In 1971 the Feltrin Manufacturing Company of Waldwick, New Jersey, makers of water coolers, moved to Harrisville, taking the place of the by then defunct Cheshire Mills. *Opposite:* Shaker Barn, Hancock, Massachusetts, c. 1827. "Buildings, mouldings and cornices, which are *merely* for *fancy,* may not be made by believers," Father Joseph Meacham wrote in the *Millennial Laws* of the Shakers.

Above: General view of the Amoskeag Mills, Manchester, New Hampshire, 1840 and afterward. The Amoskeag mills and housing are scheduled to be demolished. *Left:* Housing, Amoskeag Mills, Manchester, New Hampshire, c. 1840.

Above: ALEXANDER PARRIS, Quincy Market, Boston, Massachusetts, 1826. This is per-haps the greatest monument to the Greek Revival in Boston. Another prominent ex-ample is Parris's Stone Temple in Quincy. *Opposite, top:* ALEXANDER PARRIS, residence of David Sears (later the Somerset Club), Boston, Massachusetts, 1816. Sears, the son of one of the most successful merchants of the Federal era, was among those who fi-nanced the building of St. Paul's, the Episcopal Cathedral. *Bottom:* ALEXANDER PARRIS, St. Paul's Cathedral, Boston, Massachusetts, 1820. Although the Greek Revival did not become nationally popular until the 1830s, Parris did not hesitate to turn to Greece at this early date for the inspiration for this church.

Opposite: ELIAS CARTER, residence of Levi A. Dowley, Worcester, Massachusetts, 1842. The house, now serving Worcester Junior College, has lost some of its decorative carving, including an eagle over the front door. Dowley was a leather merchant. *Above:* ISAIAH ROGERS, Tremont House, Boston, Massachusetts, 1829. Demolished. *Photo by New-York Historical Society from A Description of the Tremont House, Boston, 1830.* "It has more galleries, colonnades, piazzas and passages than I can remember, or the reader would believe," said Dickens of his stay in this hotel.

Above: Louisburg Square, Boston, Massachusetts, c. 1840. The bow-fronts of the square, like the bow-front of the Sears house, tell how deeply Bostonians revered the architecture of the Regency in England. *Opposite:* "The Three Bricks," Nantucket, Massachusetts, 1837. These were built for the three sons of Joseph Starbuck — William, Matthew and George.

Above: Gothic cottage, Oak Bluffs, Martha's Vineyard, Massachusetts, c. 1868. The Gothic Revival lingered on in this summer colony long after it was the fashion to build in the mansardic style. *Opposite:* ALEXANDER JACKSON DAVIS, residence of W. J. Rotch, New Bedford, Massachusetts, 1850. Rotch was one of the mill owners of New Bedford.

Opposite, top: RUSSELL WARREN, residence of Levi Gale, Newport, Rhode Island, 1834. This Greek Revival mansion, now serving as a community house for Congregation Jeshuat Israel across the street, is one of many advertisements of the talent of Russell Warren, who, with James Bucklin, designed the Arcade still standing in Providence. *Bottom:* ALEXANDER JACKSON DAVIS, residence of Prescott Hall, Newport, Rhode Island, 1848. According to legend, the stones of the eighteenth-century mansion of Godfrey Malbone were incorporated in this summer house for the New York attorney Prescott Hall. *Above, top:* RICHARD UPJOHN, "Kingscote," residence of George Noble Jones, Newport, Rhode Island, 1839. Jones, the son-in-law of the Robert Hallowell Gardiner for whom Upjohn did "Oaklands," in Gardiner, Maine, was the great-grandson of Noble Wymberly Jones of "Wormslow Plantation" in Savannah. This Gothic cottage testifies to the attraction of Newport for Southerners before the Civil War. Note the "Shingle Style" wing to the left added in 1880 by McKim, Mead & White, who also did the interior room shown on page 158. *Below:* Residence of J. P. White, Belfast, Maine, c. 1840. The James Patterson White who built this Greek Revival mansion was a shipowner who served as Belfast's mayor.

Above: Richard Upjohn, "Oaklands," residence of R. H. Gardiner, Gardiner, Maine, 1835-36. Gardiner, born Robert Hallowell — he assumed the surname Gardiner to comply with the provisions of a will — was an agriculturalist who spent two years in France and England studying the science of farm management. His Gothic domain might have charmed Jane Austen, the Jane Austen who asked in *Northanger Abbey:* "Have you a stout heart? — Nerves fit for sliding panels and tapestry?" *Opposite:* "Wedding Cake House," Kennebunk, Maine, c. 1850. The Gothic slip cover was apparently added a good forty years after the original, demure, brick house was built in 1810.

HENRY AUSTIN, "Victoria Mansion," residence of Ruggles Sylvester Morse, Portland, Maine, 1859-63. Exterior and two interiors. Morse was a New Orleans hotel owner who appreciated the climate of Portland in the summer months. Open. Victoria Society of Maine. The Italian artist Giovanni Guidirini, from New York, was the artist-decorator in charge of the interior.

Below: AMMI B. YOUNG, Capitol, Montpelier, Vermont, 1836. Young, who served his apprenticeship in the office of Alexander Parris, in later years abandoned the Grecian style of the Capitol for the more solid, Italianate manner in which he designed countless post offices and custom houses in the 1850s. *Opposite:* T. R. DAKE, Ransom House, Castleton, Vermont, c. 1840. Dake was one of the more popular practitioners of the Greek Revival in Vermont.

Above: "Athenwood," residence of Thomas Waterman Wood, Montpelier, Vermont, 1850. Wood, a local artist whose paintings are preserved in the Kellogg-Hubbard Library Building in Montpelier, may have been his own architect. *Opposite, top:* Residence of W. Y. Soper, South Royalton, Vermont, c. 1850. This is a typical example of the Gothic as rendered by the carpenters of the smaller towns. It has not been possible to identify the original owner; Mr. Soper occupied it in the later nineteenth century. *Bottom:* Town Hall, Royalton, Vermont, 1840. Innovations like the Gothic and Greek Revivals were too fancy to please the carpenters who laid out this town hall.

CALEB LAMSON, contractor, covered bridge, West Dummerston, Vermont, 1872. Today the longest covered highway bridge in

Vermont still in use, it exhibits the truss patented by Ithiel Town of New Haven in 1820.

V

That Rather Low Instinct:

THE AGE OF EXUBERANCE: 1865-1901

FROM THE DEATH OF LINCOLN to the day Theodore Roosevelt entered the White House the millionaires of America were the folk heroes of the American people. This is quite understandable: the men we elected president faded easily into the wall paper of whatever rooms they entered.

Of course, the millionaire as folk hero was a notion difficult to digest for certain New Englanders. "Indeed," wrote Charles Francis Adams, Jr., who had come up against Jay Gould while managing the Union Pacific, "as I approach the end, I am more than a little puzzled to account for the instances I have seen of business success — money getting. It comes from rather a low instinct. . . . I have known, and known tolerably well, a great many *successful men, big* financially, men famous during the last half century, and a less interesting crowd I do not care to encounter. Not one that I have ever known would I care to meet again either in this world or the next, nor is one associated in my mind with the idea of humor, thought or refinement."

If Adams had gone into greater detail, he would have had to confess that Jay Gould did know how to play jokes: when he took command of the Union Pacific, which had been one of the Gould properties, he discovered a floating debt of $10,000,000 whose origin was most mysterious. And then Gould's old partner James Fisk, Jr. was known to be an outlandish humorist. "If the printing press don't break down," Fisk boasted at the height of his and Gould's campaign to oust Commodore Vanderbilt from the Erie Railroad by issuing spurious securities, "we'll give the old hog all he wants."

It was an exuberant era from Abraham Lincoln to Theodore Roosevelt, and in architecture it could be called the Age of Indiscretion. But vulgarity is al-ways more desirable than timidity, and the uninhibited exhibitionism of many of the buildings is more than welcome today when we are suffering from the blight of the "good taste" produced by so many impersonal modern architects.

Two trends may be observed in all the splendid confusion. There was a vogue for mansard roofs, which was the American way of saluting the glories of the Second Empire in France. Then there was the sudden and unmistakable revival of interest in the Venetian Gothic. This was due to the influence of John Ruskin, whose preaching was revered as deeply in the United States as in England. The Connecticut Capitol by Richard Michell Upjohn is one example of Ruskin triumphant. Still another is Mark Twain's alarming mansion at Hartford. But for Ruskin's teaching, architect Edward Tuckerman Potter might not have conceived of the polychromy of the brick walls.

The Venetian (or Ruskinian) Gothic remains in New England may be admired for themselves. They also speak eloquently of the protest against the Renaissance that was to lead to the great modern architecture of the twentieth century. Henry Van Brunt, the devoted Ruskinian who collaborated with William R. Ware on Harvard's Memorial Hall, went on to translate Viollet-le-Duc's *Discourses on Architecture*. This French text, using the cathedrals of the Middle Ages to prove that walls might be as thin as silk, was an inspiration to the Americans who created the first skyscrapers.

The great hotels of the Age of Exuberance make their own immodest claim on the attention of twentieth-century travelers who refuse to be satisfied with the humility of motels.

den pavilion, residence of Trenor W. Park, later the residence of Park's -in-law John G. McCullough, Governor of Vermont, North Bennington, Vermont, 1865. The mansion and its gardens have been opened by the McCullough-Park Foundation.

PASSENGERS
OF THE
MAY FLOWER.

JOHN TURNER, AND TWO SONS
JOHN CRACKSTON, AND SON JOHN
MOSES FLETCHER.
JOHN GOODMAN.
FRANCIS EATON, WIFE, AND SON
SAMUEL.
JAMES CHILTON, WIFE AND DAUGHTER
MARY.
DECORY PRIEST.
THOMAS WILLIAMS.
EDWARD MARGESON.
PETER BROWNE.
EDWARD FULLER, WIFE AND SON
SAMUEL.
WILLIAM MULLINS, WIFE, AND CHILDREN
JOSEPH AND PRISCILLA
EDWARD TILLEY AND WIFE.
FRANCIS COOKE AND SON JOHN
THOMAS TINKER, WIFE AND SON
JOHN RICDALE AND WIFE.
JOHN TILLEY, WIFE AND DAUGHTER
ELIZABETH.
ELLEN MOORE.
JASPER MOORE.
RICHARD MOORE AND BROTHER.
DESIRE MINTER.
WILLIAM WHITE, WIFE AND SONS
RESOLVED AND PERECRINE.
SOLOMON PROWER.
ELIAS STORY.
EDWARD THOMPSON,
ROCER WILDER.

ROBERT CUSHMAN, WHO CHARTERED
THE MAY FLOWER AND WAS ACTIVE AND
PROMINENT IN SECURING THE SUCCESS OF
THE PILCRIM ENTERPRISE, CAME IN
THE FORTUNE 1621.

MORALITY

JUSTICE

Opposite: Hammatt Billings, Pilgrim Monument, Plymouth, Massachusetts, 1859-89. Billings, who was nothing if not conscientious, hired the greatly talented William Rimmer to work with him on this commission, but Rimmer was not allowed to express himself. *Below:* Larkin Goldsmith Mead, tomb of James Fisk, Jr., Brattleboro, Vermont, c. 1872. Fisk, murdered January 7, 1872, on the staircase of the Grand Central Hotel, New York City, by one Edward S. Stokes, the lover of his last mistress, Josie Mansfield, was a native of Bennington, Vermont. But Brattleboro raised the money for this statue by the brother of Stanford White's partner William Rutherford Mead. To Brattleboro, Fisk remained one of the princes of the Erie Railroad, which he, Jay Gould and Daniel Drew had so often debauched.

117

Opposite: Pavilion Hotel, Montpelier, Vermont, 1876. This mansarded hotel was so dear to the citizens of Montpelier that in 1970 it was rebuilt (with an iron frame) to be used as a state office building. *Above:* Crawford House, Crawford Notch, New Hampshire, 1859 and later. There is a slight suspicion of Gothic Revival in the narrow mullioned windows of this famous hotel, but there is also a hint of the Colonial Revival of the late '80s in the building's present appearance.

119

C.M.F. LIBRARY

Opposite, top: Poland Spring Hotel, Poland Spring, Maine, 1876. The old hotel has been closed, and guests now stop in other buildings on the Poland Spring grounds. *Below:* CHARLES AILING GIFFORD, Mount Washington Hotel, Bretton Woods, New Hampshire, 1902. A certain sophistication was considered desirable in hotel architecture by the beginning of the twentieth century. *Above:* DETLEF LIENAU, residence of Legrand Lockwood, Norwalk, Connecticut, 1868. Lienau, a native of Schleswig-Holstein, studied under Henri Labrouste in Paris before coming to America in 1848. In 1851 he is said to have designed the first mansarded town house in New York City. His client, Legrand Lockwood, was treasurer of the Lake Shore & Michigan Southern from 1866 to 1870. When he died in 1872, he was still embarrassed by the Gold Corner of 1869 engineered by Jay Gould. His widow could not pay off the mortgage he contracted, and in 1874 there was a foreclosure on this rich mansarded mansion. Open. Lockwood-Mathews Mansion Museum of Norwalk.

Opposite: GRIDLEY J. F. BRYANT & ARTHUR GILMAN, City Hall, Boston, Massachusetts, 1865. Closeup. One of the greater mansarded city halls, this may be compared to that of Philadelphia by John McArthur. *Below:* N. J. BRADLEE (?), housing on West Canton Street, Boston, Massachusetts, c. 1860. The attribution to Bradlee is based on the likeness between these houses in the New South End and certain drawings recently issued by Walter Muir Whitehill. The New South End may have been far superior as city planning to the Back Bay, which was being filled in about the same time to permit the extension of Commonwealth Avenue and other fashionable streets. However, the New South End did not catch on, perhaps because it was on the other side of the Boston & Albany tracks. Why is it, asked Phillips Brooks, that all the mediums live in the New South End? In the last few years a wise effort has been made to reclaim this neglected section of Boston.

C.M.F. LIBRARY

Above: RICHARD MORRIS HUNT, residence of Henry Gurdon Marquand, Newport, Rhode Island, 1872. "He bought like an Italian prince of the Renaissance," wrote critic Russell Sturgis of H. G. Marquand, the railroad financier who became president of the board of trustees of the Metropolitan Museum. At this time Richard Morris Hunt was a hesitant architect, not having discovered the solution to the problem of the millionaire's palace. *Opposite:* Ware & Van Brunt, Memorial Hall, Harvard University, Cambridge, Massachusetts, 1875. Memorial Hall has lost its tower. In its best days it was a remarkable advertisement, with its polychromy, of America's devotion to the writings of John Ruskin. Henry Van Brunt was the Ruskinian who translated Viollet-le-Duc's *Discourses on Architecture.*

RICHARD MICHELL UPJOHN, Capitol, Hartford, Connecticut, 1878. Once acclaimed as one of the ten greatest buildings in the United States, this monument by the son of Richard Upjohn is one more indication of how carefully John Ruskin was read in the United States.

EDWARD TUCKERMAN POTTER, residence of Samuel L. Clemens, Hartford, Connecticut, 1874. Exterior and interiors. Potter, whose brother and uncle were both bishops of the Episcopal Church, must have enjoyed the Ruskinian polychromy of the Mark Twain house even more than his many ecclesiastical commissions. Mark Twain, so his friend William Dean Howells has told us, liked to sit up late whenever Howells occupied the royal chamber on the ground floor, "he smoking the last of his interminable cigars, and soothing his tense nerves with a mild hot scotch, while we both talked and talked. . . . After two days of this talk I would come away hollow, realizing myself best in the image of one of those locust shells which you find sticking to the bark of trees at the end of summer." Louis Comfort Tiffany was asked to decorate the interior in 1881. His work has been restored with the utmost sensitivity by the Nook Farm—Mark Twain Memorial. Open.

VI

Boston Could Be Cordial:

THE AGE OF RICHARDSON: 1872-1900

RICHARDSON IS OFF ALONE on his long journey," reflected Phillips Brooks, rector of Boston's Trinity Church, on learning of the architect's death on April 27, 1886, "I wonder how long it is."

No one could appreciate Henry Hobson Richardson more completely than the rector of the church which was his greatest monument. "He grew simpler as he grew older and greater," Brooks commented. "I have heard one of his own profession call him *barbaric*. It was that which made his work delightful."

Brooks knew all about the gifts that Richardson brought to Boston. *Why* they were brought to Boston is an interesting question, best answered by explaining what Boston had to offer him.

In Richardson's time the Episcopal Church was flourishing: Trinity could not have been built but for the support of former Unitarians eager to recognize the error of their ways. Brooks himself, the son of one-time Unitarian parents, was superb when it came to leading sectaries to the baptismal fount.

Secondly, Harvard College, from which Richardson was graduated in 1859, was transformed ten years later by Charles W. Eliot from a merely provincial institution into the great university of the western hemisphere. The Harvard faculty became unrivaled: Henry Adams was argued into teaching history for a time, and with William James, Charles Sanders Peirce, Josiah Royce and George Santayana arguing over philosophy, America listened. Two of the buildings in which the faculty enlightened the young were designed by Richardson, who came to count on the friends he made at Harvard for his best commissions.

Finally, there was the money of Boston. No architect in his right mind would think of settling in a city that was not prosperous. Boston was prosperous, and even though no businessman emerged who could compete with Cornelius Vanderbilt or Jay Gould in terrifying the stock market, the art of investing was understood. There was the younger John Murray Forbes, who knew a good thing when he saw it, and quietly presided over the destiny of the Burlington Railroad. Then there were the wise men, headed by Alexander Agassiz, son of the Swiss geologist at Harvard, who made the most out of the copper mines of Michigan's Upper Peninsula. The Calumet and Hecla mining companies were consolidated in 1871, to the very great relief of Henry Lee Higginson who was married to Alexander Agassiz's sister and, as a partner in Lee, Higginson & Co., had a wholesome interest in dividends.

Higginson, whose mansion on Beacon Street — now destroyed — was designed by Richardson, cast a particularly benign shadow on the Boston of his time. Dedicated as was no one else to the future of the Boston Symphony Orchestra, this philanthropist was a fund raiser the like of whom has not been seen in the twentieth century. Whenever Harvard was in need of another $100,000, he got it, either from a relative or from some unsuspecting citizen he persuaded into making a good impression. Perhaps Higginson should be forgiven his naive moments. "Princeton is not wicked," he called out to Harvard men at the dedication of the Soldier's Field he fought for for so long. "Yale is not base. Mates, the Princeton and the Yale fellows are our brothers."

Richardson came to the Boston of Higginson from

Louisiana, and it is to Boston's credit that no one, apparently, held it against him that he failed to fight in the Civil War. "He was a Southerner," Brooks insisted, "and nobody can understand him or his career who does not keep this fact always in mind. . . . He kept to the end much of the spirit of the Southerner before and during the Rebellion, a spirit of recklessness and earnestness, which were often strangely and strikingly combined."

Boston could put up with both recklessness and earnestness, as Richardson discovered in 1872 when he won the competition for Trinity Church. This granite building, the simplicity of whose massing suggests that he had studied the warehouses along the Boston waterfront as carefully as any of the Romanesque churches he had grown to love in France, immediately established him as the architect to bring order out of the chaos of the Age of Exuberance without sacrificing for an instant the vitality inherent in the work of his less extraordinary contemporaries.

The time had come for the Harvard men of his generation to come to his support. They did. Frederick L. Ames of the Class of 1854 was to ask him to plan practically the whole town of North Easton, Massachusetts — the railroad station, the town hall, the town library, and the gate lodge to his own mansion (the mansion itself was never built). Robert Treat Paine, who was graduated in 1855 as was Phillips Brooks, was so deeply impressed by Trinity, whose building committee he headed, that he had Richardson design a house for himself, an ex-Unitarian who could count on the dividends of Calumet & Hecla. Henry Adams of the Class of 1858 should be omitted from this list, for the house he had built by Richardson was in Washington, D. C. But James A. Rumrill of the Class of 1859 cannot be forgotten. When he got control of the Boston & Albany, he saw to it that his classmate had the chance to practice his art on a number of suburban railway stations.

So Richardson was launched, and he transformed the architecture not only of New England but of the entire United States in the late nineteenth century. The example of his public buildings was overwhelming, as was the standard he set in private houses. With the Watts Sherman house in Newport of 1874 and the M. F. Stoughton house in Cambridge of 1882 he began what the architectural historians usually refer to as the "Shingle Style." Here again the simplification of the massing was a challenge to all architects who thought in the "nervous" terms of the Age of Exuberance. And since he was careful to express the nature of the materials he used, and could plan informally for informal families, he was one of the prophets that Frank Lloyd Wright revered in Oak Park, Illinois, when he set up his own office.

A reflection of the "Shingle Style" may be perceived in the round barn of the Southwick family at East Calais, Vermont, dating from 1900. At an earlier date Henry Rutgers Marshall was following in Richardson's footsteps when he came to plan the country house of Rudyard Kipling. So was William R. Emerson in his work in the Boston suburbs. So was Clarence Luce. So was John Calvin Stevens. And so was the firm of Babb, Cook & Willard.

But no one came closer than McKim, Mead & White to understanding what Richardson accomplished. This may have been because McKim and White had served their apprenticeship in his office. Or perhaps because they were architects of Richardson's own rank. They took the "Shingle Style" of their master and made of it an even greater work of art.

McKim's Low house at Bristol, now destroyed, seems to have transfixed Frank Lloyd Wright: it was obviously the model he had in mind when he designed in 1889 the studio in Oak Park in which he began his career.

131

Opposite: H. H. RICHARDSON, Trinity Church, Boston, Massachusetts, 1872-77. The porch was added after the architect's death by Shepley, Rutan & Coolidge, the firm that succeeded to his business. Although the tower of Trinity slightly resembles that of the Cathedral of Salamanca (completed in the beginning of the sixteenth century), and although the porch does recall Saint-Gilles-du-Gard, Trinity is no exercise in archeology, and to speak of the "Richardsonian Romanesque" is to forget all about Richardson's powers of invention. Inside, Richardson collaborated with John LaFarge, who provided stained glass windows, as did William Morris and Burne-Jones. This photograph was taken before the poured concrete plaza by Sasaki, Dawson, De May Associates was thought of, and before I. M. Pei began building the sixty-story Hancock Tower to the rear. The money spent on the plaza could have been used to preserve from demolition the "Richardsonian" S. S. Pierce Building on the corner of Dartmouth Street and Huntington Avenue. Although the S. S. Pierce Building, by S. Edwin Tobey, was no masterpiece, it did relate Trinity to the Boston Public Library across the way. *Below:* H. H. RICHARDSON, Rectory, Trinity Church, Boston, Massachusetts, 1879-81. A third story was added to the original building.

Opposite, top: H. H. RICHARDSON, Cheney Building, Hartford, Connecticut, 1875. The success of this business block, now Fox's department store, made it that much easier for Richardson to obtain the commission for the Marshall Field wholesale store in Chicago. *Bottom:* H. H. RICHARDSON, Seaver Hall, Harvard University, Cambridge, Massachusetts, 1878-80. *This page, top:* H. H. RICHARDSON, Fenway Bridge, Boston, Massachusetts, 1879-81. At this time the great landscape architect, Frederick Law Olmsted, famous for Central Park, New York, was at work on the Boston parkways. *Below:* H. H. RICHARDSON, Austin Hall, Harvard University, Cambridge, Massachusetts, 1881-83. This was built for the law school, newly reorganized by Charles W. Eliot.

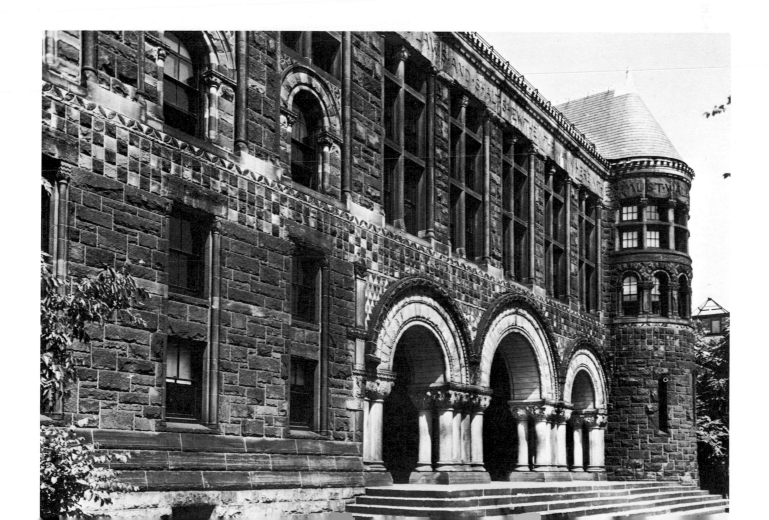

Above: H. H. Richardson, Billings Memorial Library, University of Vermont, Burlington, Vermont, 1883-85. *Opposite:* H. H. Richardson, Oliver Ames Free Library, North Easton, Massachusetts, 1879-81. Interior and exterior. The Ames family were Richardson's most important patrons. Their fortune may be said to have begun in 1844 when Oakes Ames and his brother Oliver Ames II (to whom this library is dedicated) took over the family shovel business. Following the California gold rush, the shovel business boomed and the Ameses went on to invest their profits in the Crédit Mobilier that helped finance the Union Pacific. Oakes Ames, who was sent to Congress, was censured for sharing "advantageous opportunities" with his fellow Congressmen, but Wendell Phillips, who was an exacting crusader, found that he was "one of the most honest, patriotic, devoted and far-sighted men that Massachusetts has lent to the national councils in our day." The library was donated by Oliver Ames's children, Frederick Lothrop Ames and Helen Angier Ames. The sculpture above the fireplace is the work of Augustus Saint-Gaudens. The fireplace was designed by Stanford White while he was in Richardson's office.

Above: H. H. RICHARDSON, Oliver Ames Memorial Town Hall, North Easton, Massachusetts, 1879. This was another gift of Oliver Ames's children. The landscaping and the rockery nearby were entrusted to Frederick Law Olmsted. *Opposite, top:* H. H. RICHARDSON, Gate Lodge, residence of Frederick Lothrop Ames, North Easton, Massachusetts, 1880-81. Olmsted was then at work on the landscaping of the estate. *Below:* H. H. RICHARDSON, Boston & Albany Railroad Station, Chestnut Hill, Massachusetts, 1884. Although this was the most graceful and most simple of all his railroad stations, it has been demolished.

139

Above: H. H. RICHARDSON, Old Colony Railroad Station, North Easton, Massachusetts, 1881-82. This was the gift of Frederick Lothrop Ames to the railroad of which he was a director. *Opposite:* H. H. RICHARDSON, New Haven Railroad Station, New London, Connecticut, 1885.

Opposite, top: H. H. RICHARDSON, Crane Memorial Library, Quincy, Massachusetts, 1880-83. *Bottom:* H. H. RICHARDSON, residence of Mrs. M. F. Stoughton, Cambridge, Massachusetts, 1882-83. The second story of the service wing was remodeled by Mrs. Stoughton's son, the historian John Fiske. *Above:* H. H. RICHARDSON, interior, residence of Robert Treat Paine, Waltham, Massachusetts, 1884-86.

Opposite: H. H. RICHARDSON, residence of W. Watts Sherman, Newport, Rhode Island, 1874-76. The service wing to the left was the later work of Dudley Newton. In 1973 the house is serving as an old people's home for the Baptist Church. *Above:* SHEPLEY, RUTAN & COOLIDGE, detail, Ames Building, Boston, Massachusetts, 1889.

SHEPLEY, RUTAN & COOLIDGE, residence of Albert W. Nickerson, Dedham, Massachusetts, 1886. In 1973 occupied by Noble & Greenough School, this was built for the president of the Arlington Mills in Lawrence.

Opposite: CLARENCE S. LUCE, residence of W. H. Wesson, Springfield, Massachusetts, 1882-84. In 1973 a Jewish community center, this was built for the great arms manufacturer of Springfield. *Right:* JOHN CALVIN STEVENS, residence of James Hopkins Smith, Falmouth Foreside, Maine, c. 1886. *Above:* BABB, COOK & WILLARD, Ciampolini-Atwater house, New Haven, Connecticut, 1892. There is a hint of the oncoming Colonial Revival in this house by the architects of Andrew Carnegie's mansion in New York City.

149

Above: HENRY RUTGERS MARSHALL, "Naulahka," residence of Rudyard Kipling, Dummerston, Vermont, 1892-93. Kipling was 26, and just married to the American girl, Caroline Balestier, when he began building this house where he wrote the two *Jungle Books* and *Captains Courageous. Opposite:* WILLIAM RALPH EMERSON, residence of Charles Greeley Loring, Pride's Crossing, Massachusetts, 1881. A distant cousin of Ralph Waldo Emerson, William Ralph Emerson was born in Alton, Illinois, but grew up in Boston and on the Maine coast. Beginning in 1874, he was practicing architecture on his own in Boston where he was responsible for the Boston Arts Club building. Loring was for some time director of the Boston Museum of Fine Arts.

Above: WILLIAM RALPH EMERSON, residence of Alexander Cochrane, Pride's Crossing, Massachusetts, 1881. Cochrane was one of the original directors of the American Telephone & Telegraph Co. *Opposite:* WILLIAM RALPH EMERSON, residence of William Ralph Emerson, Milton, Massachusetts, 1886.

153

Left: McKim, Mead & White, residence of Frances Skinner, Newport, Rhode Island, 1882. *Right:* Southwick family barn, East Calais, Vermont, c. 1900. This round barn in the "Shingle Style" would not be out of place near the Skinner house at Newport.

MCKIM, MEAD & WHITE, Newport Casino, Newport, Rhode Island, 1881. Pavilion, Bellevue Avenue façade, and detail of woodwork. The Casino was built to please James Gordon Bennett, Jr., the irresponsible publisher of *The New York Herald*, who became furious when the Newport Reading Room rescinded a visitor's card granted to a British friend of Bennett's who persisted in riding a horse into the Reading Room. After the top photograph was taken, a fire greatly damaged the Casino, and the pavilion (not the work of McKim, Mead & White) has disappeared.

Above, top: MCKIM, MEAD & WHITE, "Kingscote," Newport, Rhode Island, 1880. Interior. Louis Comfort Tiffany collaborated with McKim, Mead & White on this dining room. For the exterior, see page 103. *Below:* MCKIM, MEAD & WHITE, residence of Isaac Bell, Newport, Rhode Island, 1883. Bell was the brother-in-law of James Gordon Bennett, Jr. *Opposite, top:* MCKIM, MEAD & WHITE, "Southside," residence of Robert Goelet, Newport, Rhode Island, 1883. Robert Goelet, brother of the Ogden Goelet for whom Hunt did "Ochre Court," was the nephew of Peter Goelet who accumulated a great fortune in New York City real estate while minding the peacocks and storks which were his unique extravagance. *Bottom:* MCKIM, MEAD & WHITE, "Naumkeag, residence of Joseph Hodges Choate, Stockbridge, Massachusetts, 1885. Choate, who ultimately represented the United States at the Court of St. James, was a brilliant lawyer, preserving us in 1895 from the indignity of an income tax by arguing that "in striking at the corporations, in attempting to confiscate their property, you injure, not the wealthy — they can now stand it — but the widow and the orphan." Open. Trustees of Reservations.

McKim, Mead & White, residence of W. G. Low, Bristol, Rhode Island, 1887. The greatest of all the "Shingle Style" designs, the Low house was the work of McKim. It was recently destroyed, the new owner of the property having decided that it was not sufficiently "modern."

VII

There Was No Need For Sentiment:

THE GOLDEN AGE: 1872-1913

ON REACHING NEWPORT," Consuelo Vanderbilt wrote in her autobiography, "my life became that of a prisoner, with my mother and my governess as wardens. I was never out of their sight. Friends called but were told I was not at home." She was describing the last summer she spent in "Marble House," her mother's palace. Her mother, Mrs. W. K. Vanderbilt, was a woman of determination. She had decided that her daughter must marry the ninth Duke of Marlborough. "It was in the comparative quiet of an evening at home," Consuelo wrote, "that Marlborough proposed to me in the Gothic Room whose atmosphere was so propitious to sacrifice. There was no need for sentiment."

When the wedding took place, and the Duke, settled in an observation car of the private train the Vanderbilts placed at his disposal, began reading the congratulatory telegrams, it was evident that one of the summits of America's Golden Age had been reached.

The Golden Age may be said to reach from 1872, when the slight income tax imposed to pay for part of the Civil War was removed, to 1913 when the sixteenth amendment to the Constitution made possible the income tax of today. This was the era when the great millionaires founded what looked like dynasties, and when the palaces were created for the scions of these dynasties.

Consuelo's mother was something of an authority on this subject. When she married one of the Commodore's grandsons in 1875, she was dismayed to find that the proper reverence was not paid to her rank as a Princess of the New York Central Railroad: Mrs. Astor failed to leave her calling card. For this situation Mrs. Vanderbilt discovered a remedy. On March 26, 1883 she gave the grandest party in the history of New York in her palace designed by Richard Morris Hunt at 660 Fifth Avenue. One of Mrs. Astor's daughters foolishly supposed that she was automatically invited. She was quickly reminded of her error, and soon Mrs. Astor's card was left at the Vanderbilts' door.

Hunt, who solved the problem of the millionaire's palace by returning to the Renaissance for his inspiration, was not exactly neglected in Newport. For the Ogden Goelets he created "Ochre Court," a château recalling the wonders of the Loire Valley. For W. K. Vanderbilt's brother Cornelius Vanderbilt II he provided "The Breakers," whose origins have been sought in the Genoa of the Renaissance. And for Mrs. W. K. Vanderbilt herself he designed "Marble House," the rear of which proved that he made a careful study of Jules-Hardouin Mansart's Grand Trianon at Versailles.

In the meantime McKim, Mead & White, who had gone so far in the direction of modern architecture, altered their approach and rediscovered the Renaissance for themselves. Stanford White, who could be quite as magnificent as Hunt, but seldom forgot to make his interiors livable, outdid Hunt in 1902 with "Rosecliff," the terra-cotta incarnation of the Grand

RICHARD MORRIS HUNT, gates, "Ochre Court," Newport, Rhode Island, 1889-91.

Trianon which was the summer home of Hermann Oelrichs and his wife, the daughter of James Graham Fair of the Comstock Lode.

Although Edith Wharton was even more of a New Yorker than the Goelets or the Vanderbilts, she did not find Newport to her taste. For some time, before she set up her permanent residence in France, she spent the summers at Lenox, where she called upon her old friend Ogden Codman to design "The Mount" in the proper Renaissance manner. She was a demanding client. She was certain that architecture and decoration could be improved by following the best models. These were to be found "in buildings erected in Italy after the beginning of the sixteenth century, and in other European countries after the full assimilation of the Italian influence."

163

"Ochre Court," exterior and interior. In 1972, the palace of the Ogden Goelets houses Salve Regina College.

RICHARD MORRIS HUNT, "The Breakers," residence of Cornelius Vanderbilt II, New port, Rhode Island, 1892-95. Exterior and dining room. Open. Preservation Society o Newport County.

RICHARD MORRIS HUNT, "Marble House," residence of William K. Vanderbilt, Newport, Rhode Island, 1892. Gold Room, dining room and exterior. Open. Preservation Society of Newport County. The portrait of Louis XIV, in the dining room, has been attributed to Pierre Mignard.

Left: McKim, Mead & White, Boston Public Library, 1887-1895. John Singer Sargent, Edwin Austin Abbey and Puvis de Chavannes were persuaded by McKim to decorate the walls of the upper floor, the delivery room and the main corridor. *Above:* Frederick W. MacMonnies, Bacchante, c. 1887. *Photo Courtesy Metropolitan Museum of Art.* McKim intended to present this piece of sculpture to the Library, but Charles Eliot Norton, Professor of Fine Arts at Harvard, who maintained that art had ceased to exist in the year 1600, led a campaign of prudes protesting against something so suggestive in a public place, and McKim finally gave the Bacchante to the Metropolitan.

171

Above: Augustus Saint-Gaudens, Robert Gould Shaw Memorial, Boston, Massachusetts, 1897. With the aid of McKim, Saint-Gaudens designed this important monument to the memory of the Bostonian who died in the Civil War leading the Negroes of the Fifty-fourth Massachusetts. *Right:* McKim, Mead & White, residence of G. A. Nickerson, Boston, Massachusetts, 1895. This town house was evidently inspired by the David Sears house of Alexander Parris. *Opposite:* McKim, Mead & White, residence of E. D. Morgan, Newport, Rhode Island, 1891. Shore view, from one side, and entrance. Morgan was the grandson of New York's Civil War governor.

173

McKim, Mead & White, residence of Hermann Oelrichs, Newport, Rhode Island, 1902. Exterior and interior.

Above: OGDEN CODMAN, "The Mount," residence of Edith Wharton, Lenox, Massachusetts, 1902. Although Codman is said to have begun this house for the author of *Ethan Frome,* the plans — aside from a few sketches for the interior walls — are signed Hoppin & Koen, suggesting that they took over the commission. "The Mount," where Mrs. Wharton welcomed her friend Henry James, once belonged to Foxhollow School for Girls who used it as a dormitory. It is now owned by Edith Wharton Restorations and is the home of Shakespeare & Company. *Opposite, top:* CHARLES ADAMS PLATT, doorway, residence of Robert H. Schutz, Hartford, Connecticut, 1908. Platt, who could be as splendid as Hunt or McKim, Mead & White, also excelled in extremely simple and subtle Georgian houses, like this example. *Below:* CHARLES ADAMS PLATT, window detail, residence of Charles Adams Platt, Cornish, New Hampshire, c. 1900. Among those who settled near Platt in the Cornish summer colony were the novelist Winston Churchill, the sculptor Saint-Gaudens, and — for a while — the painter Thomas W. Dewing, who left on spotting the first tennis racket in the colony.

VIII

The New Look, or

MODERN TIMES

ALTHOUGH FRANK LLOYD WRIGHT owed so much to Richardson and to the early work of McKim, Mead & White, he was never to conquer New England. The very best example of his work there is the small house of Professor Theodore Baird of the Amherst faculty. And the only remarkable building of the Chicago School is the H. C. Bradley house at Woods Hole, Massachusetts. This is the work of Purcell & Elmslie, both of whom, like Wright, were graduates of the office of Louis Sullivan, the New Englander who gave Chicago its Auditorium.

The two most influential architects in the New England of the twentieth century are Ralph Adams Cram and Walter Gropius, who preached doctrines that are difficult to reconcile but were as one when it came to being dogmatic.

For Ralph Adams Cram, the Anglo-Catholic son of a Unitarian minister, the twentieth century could be dismissed as a mistake. He held that architecture was "the first of the arts to break down and disappear in the nineteenth century, maintaining itself since then only as a wistful and yet ardent effort at premeditated recovery." Richardson, whom Wright so much admired, was found wanting. "There was neither grace nor sensibility," Cram declared, "but there was power, and power was not enough." As for Frank Lloyd Wright, his contribution was dubious: "Some of the little houses of the Middle West are striking," Cram admitted, "quite novel, and inordinately clever."

Cram did not intend to be clever. By the time he began All Saints at Ashmont, Massachusetts, the church that launched his career as the prudent, archeological master of a new Gothic Revival, he knew that "the thing for me was to take up English Gothic at the point where it was cut off during the reign of Henry VIII and go on from that point, developing the style England had made her own, and along what might be assumed to be logical lines, with due regard to the changing conditions of contemporary culture."

He was impatient with the Gothic Revival of the romantic era. "Even the Dark Ages that followed the Fall of Rome could . . . show no parallel, for even then such building as was done had at least the qualities of modesty and sincerity of purpose. The black years of American architecture revealed neither of these qualities; instead the product was vulgar, self-satisfied and pretentious, instinct with frontier ideology and as rampantly individualistic as the society it so admirably expressed."

The younger generation was in need of guidance, and very few measured up to the standards on which Cram insisted. When he became Chairman of the School of Architecture at M.I.T., he made this most plain. "I took the position," he said, "that my function was not to get men into the architectural profession, but to keep them out."

The German Walter Gropius, who came from the Bauhaus to superintend Harvard's School of Architecture in 1937, was hailed as the herald of a new era; like Cram, however, he was worried if students glanced around. "When the innocent beginner," Gropius announced, "is introduced to the great achievements of the past, he may be too easily discouraged from trying to create for himself."

Not that creating *for oneself* was desirable. Gropius dreamed of the wonders that a collective society might accomplish. To this ideal he was as loyal as was Cram to the memory of King Charles the First — or Charles the Martyr as he was known to Cram and the other fervent members of the Jacobite Society "The Order of the White Rose."

"The dominant spirit of our epoch is already recognizable although its form is not yet clearly defined," Gropius discovered. "The old dualistic world-concept which envisaged the ego in opposition to the universe is rapidly losing ground. In its place is rising the idea of a universal unity in which all opposing forces exist in a state of absolute balance."

The individual could be tolerated, but only if he knew his place. "Students," Gropius decided, "should be trained to create in teams. . . . It is true," he added, "that the creative spark originates always with the individual, but by working in close collaboration with others toward a common aim, he will attain greater heights of achievement through the stimulation and challenging critique of his teammates, than by living in an ivory tower."

What teamwork could achieve was made clear in 1950 when The Architects' Collaborative, the firm that he and his most loyal students founded, produced the dining hall of the Harvard Graduate Center as well as a dormitory unit. These were undistinguished buildings. Another and more famous undistinguished building was the 1963 Pan-Am tower in New York City. Here Gropius and Pietro Belluschi, who by then had taken Cram's job at M.I.T., were pleased to collaborate with Emery Roth & Sons on a skyscraper that undid all the advances in city planning provided by the Grand Central Station.

"It is," Gropius confessed in an indiscreet moment, "just as easy to create a modern strait-jacket as a Tudor one."

Criticism was stilled in the Cambridge that Gropius dominated, and it is not surprising that neither Le Corbusier nor Alvar Aalto, both of whom had done great work in Europe, made a convincing contribution to the architecture along the Charles River. As for most of the recent buildings in and around the Harvard Yard, they tell the sad story of teamwork triumphant.

Nor is the New Look of Boston particularly rewarding. The 60-story John Hancock Tower by I. M. Pei & Partners now being completed to the rear of Trinity Church could be dismissed as just another example of the ubiquitous curtain-wall or all-glass skyscraper were it not for the damage it has done to the foundations of Trinity: the excavations for the Hancock Tower have so disturbed the fill and mud beneath the church that one corner has gone down one and one-half inches and the church tower is down approximately one and three-quarters inches.

The most advertised exhibit of recent modern architecture in Boston is, of course, the new City Hall completed in 1969 by Kallman, McKinnell & Knowles. It bears an interesting similarity to one of the great modern buildings of Europe, Le Corbusier's monastery of Sainte-Marie-de-la-Tourette at Eveux-sur-l'Arbrèsle near Lyons, and raises the question: is studying someone else's monastery the best preparation for designing your own city hall? The problems involved are different. In any event, next to no thought has been given to the convenience of the Boston public, and the exterior staircase to the rear is bound to be hazardous on winter days.

The new City Hall is hardly an original work of art, and it may be argued that originality pure and simple is not the answer to every problem. Originality is not the outstanding characteristic of the Boston Public Library by McKim, Mead & White. Its glorious façade does echo that of the Bibliothèque Sainte-Geneviève in Paris by Henri Labrouste, and one of the acknowledged ancestors of both libraries is Alberti's Church of San Francesco at Rimini. What is remarkable about McKim's library is its plan. No doubt he aimed to impress the public. There is also no doubt that he aimed and succeeded in solving certain practical problems.

The Boston Public Library and Trinity Church across the way have been ignored by Sasaki, Dawson, De May Associates, the planners of the self-conscious plaza of Copley Square. Philip Johnson, who once studied with Gropius, fortunately has shown much more consideration for McKim's library in the addition he is now completing to the rear.

And there are signs that New England is recovering from the influence of Gropius. The Yale School of Architecture may be described as a haven for those who did not subscribe to the ideal of teamwork. George Howe, once the director of the school, welcomed the casual message of the latest architecture on the West Coast when he designed in 1939 the most undoctrinaire summer home of Clara Fargo Thomas on Mount Desert Island in Maine. Paul M. Rudolph, yet another head of the Yale School, has proved he is a brilliant disciple of Le Corbusier in the new campus of the South Eastern Massachusetts Technical Institute at North Dartmouth. And Charles W. Moore, the present head, has advertised a concern for texture that Gropius could never comprehend in the cypress-sheathed house of Paul M. Klotz at Westerly, Rhode Island.

Then there is the Yale-educated Eero Saarinen. When he came to build Yale's Ingalls Hockey Rink, he could not help revealing that he was as imaginative as Gropius was sterile. He went on to lay out the new Morse and Stiles Colleges at Yale that harmonize so easily with the Tudor Gothic additions to the campus in the 1920s.

If Saarinen is not forgotten, tomorrow in New England need not repeat the mistakes of today.

179

180

Opposite, top: COOLIDGE, SHEPLEY, BULFINCH & ABBOTT, Dunster House, Harvard University, Cambridge, Massachusetts, 1930. This conservatively-designed dormitory was part of the revolutionary Harvard "house plan" introduced by President A. Lawrence Lowell; the Harvard clubs were no longer so appealing when students could easily obtain decent housing and the chance to meet all of their contemporaries. The Harvard "house plan" was financed by $10,000,000 from Edward S. Harkness, Yale '97, Yale having hesitated to accept this idea until Harvard showed the way. *Photo Harvard Publicity Bureau. Bottom:* RALPH ADAMS CRAM, All Saints Church, Ashmont, Massachusetts, 1893. *This page, top:* FRANK LLOYD WRIGHT, residence of Theodore Baird, Amherst, Massachusetts, 1940. *Below:* PURCELL & ELMSLIE, residence of H. C. Bradley, Woods Hole, Massachusetts, 1912. Bradley was the son-in-law of Charles R. Crane, the Chicagoan who backed Robert M. LaFollette for President in 1912.

Above: MARCEL BREUER, residence of Ogden Kniffin, New Canaan, Connecticut, 1948. One of Breuer's recent commissions is the Whitney Museum in New York City. *Right:* GROPIUS & BREUER, residence of Marcel Breuer, Lincoln, Massachusetts, 1939. This was one of the first examples of the "International Style" advocated by Walter Gropius and his partner from the Bauhaus days, Marcel Breuer.

184

PHILIP JOHNSON, residence of Philip Johnson, New Canaan, Connecticut, 1948. Exterior and interior (1948), and pavilion (1963). The son of one of the leading lawyers of Cleveland, Ohio, Johnson built this retreat for himself not long after his graduation from the Harvard School of Architecture. Johnson was one of the first Americans to praise Walter Gropius: as early as 1932 he featured Gropius's work in the celebrated "International Style" exhibit he staged at the Museum of Modern Art, New York. But in recent years Johnson has become bored with the dogma of the "International Style," and has even criticized Ludwig Miës van der Rohe, with whom he designed the Seagram Building in New York City. "My direction is clear; eclectic traditionalism," Johnson has conceded. "This is not academic revivalism. There are no classic orders or Gothic finials. I try to pick up what I like throughout history. We cannot *not* know history."

Top and below: LOUIS KAHN, Library, Phillips Exeter Academy, Exeter, New Hampshire, 1972. Exterior and interior. This native of Estonia offered an austere challenge to the doctrine of Walter Gropius.

Opposite, top: ALVAR AALTO, Baker House Dormitory, Massachusetts Institute of Technology, Cambridge, Massachusetts, 1949. The Baker Dormitory, which is not half so dramatic as many of Aalto's works in his native Finland, fails to show the interest in texture which makes his Finnish performances so memorable. Opposite, below: LE CORBUSIER, Carpenter Art Center, Harvard University, Cambridge, Massachusetts, 1963. Le Corbusier, who was inclined to idealize American silos while in Europe, no sooner arrived in the United States than he shocked all of the prigs in the architectural profession by paying homage to the Renaissance palaces of McKim, Mead & White.

Above: EERO SAARINEN, Kresge Auditorium, Massachusetts Institute of Technology, Cambridge, Massachusetts, 1954. The son of the Eliel Saarinen of Cranbrook, Eero was completing the General Motors Technical Center at Warren, Michigan when this commission came into the office. It allowed him to experiment in a different direction from the GM Center which showed how highly he respected Ludwig Miës van der Rohe. *Opposite:* ELIEL SAARINEN, Music Shed, Tanglewood, Lenox, Massachusetts, 1938. Exterior and interior. Saarinen, who came from Finland to head the Cranbrook Academy at Bloomfield Hills, Michigan and create Cranbrook's buildings, was selected by Sergei Koussevitzky of the Boston Symphony to plan this shed for the Symphony's summer concerts.

Above: EERO SAARINEN, Chapel, Massachusetts Institute of Technology, Cambridge, Massachusetts, 1955. Calling on Theodore Roszak to design the bell-tower and on Harry Bertoia to invent the altar screen, Saarinen was well on the way to the sculptural forms of his last commissions. *Opposite:* EERO SAARINEN, Ingalls Hockey Rink, Yale University, New Haven, Connecticut, 1955.

190

Eero Saarinen, Yale University, New Haven, Connecticut, 1961-62.
Below: Morse College; *opposite:* Stiles College.

Above: Skidmore, Owings & Merrill, Beinecke Library, Yale University, New Haven, Connecticut, 1963. The translucent library, a departure from the curtain-wall skyscrapers for which SOM is so well known, houses Yale's rare book collection. *Opposite, top:* Paul M. Rudolph, Southeastern Massachusetts Technical Institute, North Dartmouth, Massachusetts, 1963 and later. The campus, now being completed, is proof of how completely Rudolph has mastered the art of capturing sculptural forms in concrete. *Below:* Paul M. Rudolph, Parking Garage, New Haven, Connecticut, 1962. A graduate of the Harvard School of Architecture, Rudolph headed Yale's school from 1958 to 1965, making his own experiments with the poured concrete whose dramatic possibilities had already been sensed by Le Corbusier.

194

Right and opposite below: CHARLES W. MOORE, residence of Paul M. Klotz, Westerly, Rhode Island, 1969. Exterior and interior. For years the head of the Yale School, Moore is a native of Benton Harbor, Michigan, and a graduate of the University of Michigan School of Architecture. He has practised on the West Coast and is no stranger to the informality of West Coast architecture. *Below:* HARWELL HAMILTON HARRIS, residence of Gerald M. Loeb, Redding, Connecticut, 1949. Practising in 1973 in Raleigh, North Carolina, Harris is the Californian who has explored so carefully the possibilities of the tradition launched by Bernard R. Maybeck and the brothers Greene & Greene.

196

Top: WILLIAM REINECKE, residence of Harvey Sibley, Warren, Vermont, 1965-69. One of the ski lodges of the Prickley Mountain project, the Sibley house was begun by William Reinecke, just graduated from the Yale Architectural School, and completed by David Sellers and Charles Hosford. *Bottom:* GEORGE HOWE, residence of Clara Fargo Thomas, Mount Desert Island, Maine, 1939. A far from dogmatic architect in his early non-modern work in the Philadelphia suburbs, Howe had no difficulty in imagining this unaffected cottage.

Bibliography

Adams, Charles Francis, ed., *Works of John Adams*, 10 v., Boston, 1850-56.

Adams, Mary, ed., *The Lockwood-Mathews Mansion*, Norwalk, Connecticut, 1969.

Allen, A. V. G., *Life and Letters of Phillips Brooks*, 2 v., New York, 1901.

Allen, Richard Sanders, *Covered Bridges of the Northeast*, Brattleboro, Vermont, 1959.

Andrews, Edward Deming, *The People Called Shakers*, New York, 1953.

Armstrong, John Borden, *Factory under the Elms: A History of Harrisville, New Hampshire*, Cambridge, Massachusetts, 1969.

Balsan, Consuelo Vanderbilt, *The Glitter and the Gold*, New York, 1952.

Baxter, W. T., *The House of Hancock*, Cambridge, Massachusetts, 1945.

Bayer, Herbert, et al., eds., *Bauhaus 1919-1928*, New York, 1938.

Bentley, William, *Diary*, 4 v., Salem, Massachusetts, 1905.

Bridenbaugh, Carl, *Peter Harrison: First American Architect*, Chapel Hill, North Carolina, 1949.

Briggs, Martin S., *The Homes of the Pilgrim Fathers in England and America*, New York, 1932.

Brooks, Phillips, "Henry Hobson Richardson," *Harvard Monthly*, October, 1886.

Brown, Robert F., *The Architecture of Henry Hobson Richardson in North Easton, Massachusetts*, North Easton, 1969.

Bulfinch, Ellen Susan, *The Life and Letters of Charles Bulfinch*, Boston, 1896.

Bunting, Bainbridge, *Houses of Boston's Back Bay*, Cambridge, Massachusetts, 1967.

Calderwood, Cornelia L., *The Story of Victoria Mansion*, Portland, Maine, 1965.

Candee, Richard M., "Three Architects of Early New Hampshire Mill Towns," *Journal of the Society of Architectural Historians*, May, 1971.

Codman, Florence, *The Clever Young Boston Architect*, Augusta, Maine, 1970.

Congdon, Herbert Heaton, *Old Vermont Houses*, Peterborough, New Hampshire, 1968.

Coolidge, John P., *Mill and Mansion*, New York, 1942.

Coolidge, Thomas Jefferson, *An Autobiography*, Boston, 1921.

Cram, Ralph Adams, *My Life in Architecture*, Boston, 1936.

—— *The Ministry of Art*, Freeport, New York, 1967.

—— *The Substance of Gothic*, Boston, 1928.

DaCosta, Beverly, ed., *American Heritage Guide: Historic Houses*, New York, 1971.

Dexter, Franklin B., ed., *The Literary Diary of Ezra Stiles*, 3 v., New York, 1901.

Downing, Antoinette, and Scully, Vincent, Jr., *The Architectural Heritage of Newport*, Cambridge, Massachusetts, 1952.

Doyle, Mary Virginia, "John Calvin Stevens: In Pursuit of Art." Unpublished master's essay, Brown University, 1957.

Elliott, Maude Howe, *This Was My Newport*, Cambridge, Massachusetts, 1944.

Ford, Worthington C., ed., *Statesman and Friend: Correspondence of John Adams with Benjamin Waterhouse*, Boston, 1927.

Fox, Dixon Ryan, *Yankees and Yorkers*, New York, 1940.

Freeman, Donald, ed., *Boston Architecture*, Cambridge, Massachusetts, 1970.

Garvan, Anthony N. B., *Architecture and Town Planning in Colonial Connecticut*, New Haven, 1951.

Gay, Leon S., "Dwellings from the Hills," *Vermont Life*, Fall, 1950.

Giedion, Sigfried, *Walter Gropius: Work and Teamwork*, New York, 1954.

Giffen, Jane C., "The Moffatt-Ladd House," *The Connoisseur*, October and November, 1970.

Goody, Joanne E., *New Architecture in Boston*, Cambridge, Massachusetts, 1965.

Grant, Marion H., *A Guidebook to Greater Hartford, Connecticut*, Hartford, 1966.

Gratiot, Daphne A., "Woodstock's Houses: A Gracious Heritage," *Vermont Life*, Spring, 1959.

Gropius, Walter, *The New Architecture and the Bauhaus*, New York, 1936.

Hedges, James B., *The Browns of Providence Plantations: Colonial Years*, Cambridge, Massachusetts, 1952.

Hitchcock, Henry Russell, *The Architecture of H. H. Richardson and His Times*, New York, 1936.

—— *A Guide to Boston Architecture*, New York, 1954.

—— *Rhode Island Architecture*, Providence, 1939.

Howe, Mark A. de Wolfe, *Bristol*, Cambridge, Massachusetts, 1930.

Howells, John Mead, *The Architectural Heritage of the Merrimack*, New York, 1941.

—— *The Architectural Heritage of the Piscataqua*, New York, 1937.

—— *Lost Examples of Colonial Architecture*, New York, 1963.

James, Henry, *Charles W. Eliot*, 2 v., Boston, 1930.

Jameson, J. Franklin, ed., *Johnson's Wonder-working Providence*, New York, 1910.

Jordy, William H., and Coe, Ralph, eds., *American Architecture and other Writings by Montgomery Schuyler*, 2 v., Cambridge, Massachusetts, 1961.

Kelly, J. Frederick, *Early Connecticut Meeting Houses,* 2 v., New York, 1948.

Kilham, Walter H., *Boston after Bulfinch,* Cambridge, Massachusetts, 1946.

Kimball, Fiske, *Domestic Architecture of the American Colonies and the Early Republic,* New York, 1922.

—— *Mr. Samuel McIntire, Carver: The Architect of Salem,* Salem, Massachusetts, 1940.

Kimball, Gertrude S., *Providence in Colonial Times,* Boston, 1912.

Kirker, Harold, *The Architecture of Charles Bulfinch,* Cambridge, Massachusetts, 1969.

Kirker, Harold and James, *Bulfinch's Boston, 1787-1817,* New York, 1964.

Larcom, Lucy, *A New England Childhood,* New York, 1961.

Mark Twain Memorial, *Mark Twain in Hartford,* Hartford, Connecticut, 1958.

Marquand, John P., *Timothy Dexter Revisited,* Boston, 1925.

Mather, Cotton, *Magnalia Christi Americana,* 2 v., New York, 1967.

Mayo, Lawrence S., *John Langdon,* Concord, Massachusetts, 1937.

—— *John Wentworth,* Cambridge, Massachusetts, 1921.

Metz, Don, *New Architecture in New Haven,* Cambridge, Massachusetts, 1966.

Monkhouse, Christopher P., *Faneuil Hall Market: An Account of Its Many Likenesses,* Boston, 1969.

Morison, Samuel Eliot, *Harrison Gray Otis: The Urbane Federalist, 1765-1848,* Boston, 1969.

—— *The Maritime History of Massachusetts,* Boston, 1921.

Morrison, Hugh S., *Early American Architecture,* New York, 1952.

Museum of Fine Arts, Boston, *Back Bay Boston: The City as a Work of Art,* Boston, 1969.

Parsons, Francis, *The Friendly Club,* Hartford, Connecticut, 1922.

Perry, Bliss, *Life and Letters of Henry Lee Higginson,* Boston, 1921.

Place, Charles A., *Charles Bulfinch: Architect and Citizen,* Boston, 1925.

Reed, Henry Hope, *Marble House,* Newport, Rhode Island, 1965.

Rice, Howard C., "Rudyard Kipling's House in Vermont," *Vermont Life,* Spring, 1952.

Richardson, Henry Hobson, *A Description of Trinity Church,* Boston, nd.

Rogers, Mary C., *Glimpses of an Old Social Capital,* Boston, 1923.

Scully, Vincent J., Jr., *The Shingle Style: Architectural Theory and Design from Richardson to the Origins of Wright,* New Haven, Connecticut, 1955.

Shurtleff, Harold R., *The Log Cabin Myth,* Cambridge, Massachusetts, 1939.

Sigourney, Lydia Huntley, *Scenes from My Native Land,* London, 1845.

Silliman, Benjamin, *Remarks made on a short tour. . . .,* New Haven, Connecticut, 1824.

Smales, Holbert T., *The Breakers: An Illustrated Handbook,* Newport, Rhode Island, 1952.

Trowbridge, Bertha C., ed., *Old Houses of Connecticut,* New Haven, 1923.

Tuthill, Mrs. L. C., *History of Architecture from the Earliest Times,* Philadelphia, 1848.

Tutt, Hannah, *The Lee Mansion: What It Was and What It Is,* Marblehead, Massachusetts, 1911.

Van Doren, Mark, ed., *Samuel Sewall's Diary,* New York, 1927.

Van Rensselaer, Marianna G., *Henry Hobson Richardson and His Works,* Boston, 1888.

Wadsworth, Daniel, "Architecture," *American Journal of Science and Arts,* April-June, 1833.

Ware, Caroline F., *The Early New England Cotton Manufacture,* Boston, 1921.

Warren, William L., "William Sprats and His Civil and Ecclesiastical Architecture in New England," *Old-Time New England,* January-June, 1954.

Watkins, Walter Kendall, "Hancock House, Boston," *Old-Time New England,* July, 1926.

Wharton, Edith, and Codman, Ogden, *The Decoration of Houses,* New York, 1897.

White, Col. Hunter C., *Wickford and Its Old Houses,* Wickford, Rhode Island, 1947.

Whitehill, Walter Muir, *Boston: A Topographical History,* Cambridge, Massachusetts, 1959.

—— *Boston Public Library: A Centennial History,* Cambridge, Massachusetts, 1956.

Zaitzevsky, Cynthia, *The Architecture of William Ralph Emerson,* Cambridge, Massachusetts, 1969.

Index

REFERENCE